"Inspiring and uplifting—*We May Not Be Crazy, But Sometimes I Wonder* is not just a collection of humorous stories; it's a captivating exploration of what it means to live a fulfilling life. The author shares her insights and lessons learned—a powerful reminder that the most meaningful experiences often lie outside the boundaries of our expectations."

—Kelly Montgomery, social media manager

"Right from the first paragraph Lynda has the unique gift to draw you intimately into her world. I found myself howling with laughter, smiling, nodding, and looking forward to the next chapter. It was as if I had a front row seat, an invitation into "Lynda's world." Warning—once you start reading, you won't want to put it down."

—Leanne Monaghan, peak performance coach and health and fitness educator

"I first met Lynda Pilon when she attended one of the author retreats my company hosts. When I looked at her manuscript, I was impressed with her ability to tell personal stories in a very humorous way. Lynda has that rare ability to make us all laugh at life. Read her book. Better yet, buy another copy as a gift for a friend!"

—Steve Harrison, co-founder of *Author Success* and *Bradley Communications Corp.*

"A wonderful collection of memories, mayhem, and follies of a couple coping with family, retirement, and aging. Each chapter shows us that there is always room for adventure, growth, and an abundance of laughter. A must read."

—Marjorie Matthews, senior club program coordinator

"Unlike many memoirs focusing on traumatic events or an arduous search for life's purpose, this work is a delightful change. Filled with relatable vignettes, readers will revel in the author's use of these slices of time, showing life can be fun, uplifting, and filled with optimism, proving that finding humor in chaos results in laughter, resilience, and camaraderie."

—Merida Johns, Author, *Blackhorse Road, Flower Girl,* and *Flawless Witness*

"Lynda shows us that every family is normal in their own crazy way, with the gift of laughter being essential in helping to face the ups and downs of everyday life. Well written with stories everyone can relate to."

—Betty Traynor, wife, mother and grandma

WE MAY NOT BE CRAZY, BUT SOMETIMES I WONDER

Embracing Life's Journey With Humour, Wisdom and Adventure

Lynda Pilon

WE MAY NOT BE CRAZY, BUT SOMETIMES I WONDER

Embracing Life's Journey With Humour, Wisdom and Adventure

LYNDA PILON

Copyright © 2024 Lynda Pilon

All rights reserved. This book or any portion thereof may not be reproduced or used in any manner whatsoever without the express written permission of the author except for the use of brief quotations in a book review.

ISBN (paperback): 978-1-0689764-2-1
ISBN (ebook): 978-1-0689764-3-8

Book design and production by www.AuthorSuccess.com
Cover art by iStock

Printed in the United States of America

To my family, whose antics have provided endless material for this book.

CONTENTS

Introduction — 1

Chapter 1: Grandkids: A Source of Lifelong Lessons — 3
    Let the Lessons Begin — 3
    A Night to Remember — 5
    Are We Having Fun Yet? — 10
    No Plans Are the Best Plans — 14
    The Price of a Cup of Tea — 17
    The Unexpected Request — 21

Chapter 2: Tales of Sleep Deprivation — 29
    Parent Trickery — 29
    Hot Babes — 32
    It's All in The Bed — 34
    The Calm Before the Horn — 37

Chapter 3: The Golden Years — 41
    Retirement: From City Life to Country Dreams — 41
    Ma'am Is Not Home — 46
    Your Kids Don't Want Your Junk — 49
    Half the Fun is Getting There — 52
    Mind Travel: All Aboard — 55

Chapter 4: Chaos and Order: — 59
    Wild Sex in the Country — 59
    From Green Thumbs to Grocery Runs — 61
    Spraying For Divorce — 62
    Crap Happens — 64
    The Annoying Visitors — 66
    Where Do You Find a Hero? — 69

The Missing Hard Hat	72
Idiot or Genius?: That Is the Question	74

Chapter 5: Other Family Members   77

"Mom, Can We Have a Dog?"	77
From Stray to Stay	79
Consequences	84
Max, the Cat	86
Molly's House	90
Nothing Is Free	93

Chapter 6: Family Gatherings   99

That Magical Time of Year	99
The First Sign of Christmas	100
Our Memory Tree	102
Winkin' On and Blinkin' Off	104
Cha-Ching: The Sound of Christmas	105
Gift Shopping, Man Style	109
Buying for the Wife	111

Chapter 7: This Aging Thing   **115**

Wine, Women, and Wisdom	115
The Name of the Game	119
Is Mom Ready for the Home?	123
Saving One's Sole	126
Undercover Shopping	128
If All Else Fails, Just Wave	132
The Aging Test	135

INTRODUCTION

CALM AND CHAOS—that's family life. Daily existence has its ups and downs, and I have found the best way to deal with the downs is to have a sense of humour, and above all, to laugh at yourself. The trick is to look at the situation, put things in perspective, and then maybe a smile will cross your face.

Now, let's be clear—I'm not talking about the soul-crushing tragedies that life throws our way. No, I'm referring to those pesky little irritations that sneak into our daily lives—unwanted wildlife, lack of sleep, incompetent contractors—things that slowly chip away at our sanity until we're ready to explode.

Over the years, I've told friends and relatives stories about my own frustrating situations and the unorthodox methods my family and I have used to deal with them. They would smile and laugh, and invariably say something like, "Lynda, you should put these stories in a book." But writing a book seemed overwhelming. Procrastination reigned—no book, just more oral stories. Then along came COVID-19, with all its restrictions, and an unexpected opportunity presented itself to me. I suddenly had time available for new projects. It was time to *write* my stories.

To get my feet wet, I started a blog on Facebook, which I named *From the Senior's Corner*. My life's misadventures, the antics of an unpredictable yet resourceful husband, the kind but unwelcomed parenting-of-parents by middle-aged kids, and the spirited activities of grandchildren were all covered in full-blown colour.

Comments soon started coming in regarding my blog.

"I really enjoyed your story. The same thing happened to me."

"I laughed out loud. I cannot wait to read your story to my great-grandkids."

"You hit the nail on the head. I remember those times."

"I had a crappy day. I needed that laugh."

It seemed that I had hit a chord with my readers. The statement, "That which is most personal, is most universal," was ringing true. My life, with its joys and challenges, was no different from anyone else's, but the way I told my stories of everyday occurrences often left listeners nodding in agreement, grinning from ear to ear, and occasionally bursting into a hearty belly laugh. That's why I decided to put them all together in this book, *We May Not Be Crazy, But Sometimes I Wonder,* a random collection of over forty short anecdotes, where generations collide, emotions intertwine, and laughter triumphs.

Let me introduce you to my tribe: Chuck, my husband; Tammy, my daughter; Steven, my son; Dean, my son-in-law; Rowena, my daughter-in-law; and my grandchildren: Griffin, Claire, Andrew, and Mackenna. As the curtain rises on our unfiltered experiences, you may find echoes of your own lives within these pages. So, welcome to my world, where the party of life awaits.

May these tales inspire you to smile, laugh, and take yourself a little less seriously.

CHAPTER 1

GRANDKIDS: A SOURCE OF LIFELONG LESSONS

What happens at Grandma's, stays at Grandma's

Let the Lessons Begin

Have your grandchildren ever had you questioning what you say and what you do? Well, mine certainly have. You see, these precious little ones aren't just about cuteness and giggles; they're stealthy little life coaches who sneakily teach us life's greatest lessons. There was a time, pre-grandkids, when I would occasionally pepper my sentences with the odd *bad* word. But with the arrival of this new generation, I really tried to clean up my act, especially when the grandchildren were under my watch. I prided myself in being cuss-free, but apparently, one day, according to Griffin, I failed miserably at this undertaking.

It had been a long day of babysitting. Griffin and I had played in the park, attended story time at the library, and then returned to the park for one last swing before heading home. Let's face it, Grandma was tired. Griffin was not.

As the clock ticked closer to my quitting time, I informed this little bundle of energy that it was time for him to put away his toys before Mommy came home.

"I bet I can put away more toys than you," I challenged him.

The game was on. A flurry of activity followed, and soon the job was completed. As I made my way toward the kitchen, my unsuspecting foot encountered a stray Hot Wheels car that had managed to evade our clean-up efforts. With the precision of a Formula One racer, this tiny speedster darted from beneath my foot, sending me tumbling backwards with a thud that rattled even my teeth. Unfortunately, I uttered my annoyance within earshot of Griffin.

This three-year-old word enforcer looked at me with stern disapproval, brows knitted, and stated in a very disappointed voice, "Grandma, you said the *s* word."

I vehemently denied this, but my little word police officer soon set me straight.

"Grandma," he declared with great authority, "*stupid* is a bad word!"

Note to self: *oh, for Pete's sake* is now the only acceptable way to express frustration.

Now, let's dive into the realm of toddler linguistics with our two-year-old language master, Claire. Picture this: a peculiar wiggly walk that caught my attention.

Curious, I inquired, "Claire. Do you need to use the bathroom?"

To which she casually replied, "No, Grandma, it's just a wedgie."

I mean, come on, where do they learn this stuff? Grandma's vocabulary has been updated, and it's all thanks to Claire's schooling in modern lingo.

And then there's the undisputed master of time management, four-year-old Mackenna. After a marathon of babysitting, I declared a well-deserved ten-minute tea break. With the kettle singing its anthem and tea steeping like a champ, I was ready to relax.

Enter Mackenna, who promptly announced, "Alright, Grandma, time's up. Let's get cracking!"

Lesson learned: tea breaks are apparently overrated in the preschool world.

But let's not forget the comedy corner, where my grandkids have taken up residency. Eight-year-old Andrew once posed the question, "Grandma, how do you keep a turkey in suspense?"

And when I sheepishly admitted I didn't know, he fired back with, "I'll tell you tomorrow."

Cheeky, right? I'm on the edge of my seat, Andrew!

From language policing to wedgie revelations to time management and suspenseful turkey tales, I knew in my heart the wisdom, the hilarity, and the grandkid-inspired life lessons were just getting started. My grandparenting skills were evolving and flourishing, all credit due to their influence. In essence, they, like all grandchildren, held the pen to the unwritten manuscript titled *How to Keep Grandparents on Their Toes*. This journey, I realized, was an ongoing adventure, with each chapter unfolding through the unique and endearing interactions with these little authors of joy.

A Night to Remember

Have you ever experienced a day so full of excitement and anticipation that even sleep couldn't contain it? Imagine the following scene:

grandchildren—two kids aged four, and the third child aged two—a day and night of boundless energy, games, crafts, and outside activities. But best of all, with no parental supervision, the motto "What happens at Grandma's, stays at Grandma's" is strictly adhered to. It was a scenario that promised cherished memories, restful bedtime routines, and a well-deserved cup of tea for Grandma at the end of the day . . . or so I thought. But as the sun set on that eventful day, exhaustion took a surprising turn. This is how the events evolved.

The Sleepover

Claire was going to sleep over at Grandma and Grandpa's farm. Even better, her little brother Andrew and their cousin Griffin were going, too. They would all get to sleep in the same bed.

"I'm so excited," Claire informed her mother. "I can't wait!"

"Tomorrow will come soon enough. Time for sleep now," her mother said firmly.

The next day, two moms dropped off three very energized children.

"Remember, when Grandma says bedtime, it's bedtime. No excuses and no whining," said Griffin's mom.

"Be good you guys, and make sure Grandpa *behaves*," Claire and Andrew's mom added.

"I'm sure we will follow all the rules," said Grandpa, as he gave the children a sly wink.

There was so much to do. Grandpa took them on a hay ride. They fed the chipmunks and chased the squirrels. They went swimming and played on the swings. They made cupcakes with Grandma. But finally, it was after supper and time for bed.

"We aren't tired," they said.

"Well, I'm tired," said Grandpa.

"I'm exhausted," said Grandma. "So, we are all going to bed."
"Will you sleep in the room with us?" asked Griffin.
"That would be so much fun," giggled Claire.

So, Claire, Andrew, and Griffin climbed into one bed and Grandma and Grandpa climbed into the bed next to theirs.

"Tell us a story," they begged, so Grandma told them about the adventures of a little train.

When the "Choo-choo! Woo-woo!" sounds from the children had stopped, Grandma announced, "Time to sleep. Goodnight, Claire. Goodnight, Andrew. Goodnight, Griffin. Love you guys."

"Goodnight, Grandma," they said. "Goodnight, Grandpa."

But Grandpa didn't say a word. Instead, a very mischievous grin appeared on his face.

Grandpa let out loud pretend snores.

ZZZZZZZZZZZZZZZZZZZZ

The children shrieked with laughter, and immediately three more snoring sounds filled the room.

ZZZZZZZZZZZZZZZZZZZZZZZZZZZZZZ

Grandma was *not* amused.

"Oh, for Pete's sake," said Grandma. "You will never get to sleep making that noise. It is time for all snorers, big and little, to go to sleep. Goodnight!"

Grandma looked at Grandpa and gave him "*the look.*" All was quiet.

But there on Grandpa's face was that mischievous grin.

TOOT!

"Must have been the beans I had for supper," Grandpa said.

Howls of laughter filled the air as sounds of TOOT, TOOT, TOOOOOOOOOOOT were being made.

Andrew was jumping up and down on the bed. Claire was kicking her legs up in the air, and Griffin was trying to make the loudest toot noise by blowing on his arm.

Grandma was *not* amused.

"Oh, for Pete's sake," said Grandma. "You will never get to sleep making that noise. It is time for all tooters, big and little, to *go to sleep*. Goodnight."

Grandma looked at Grandpa and gave him "*the look*." All was quiet.

But once again, that mischievous grin was on Grandpa's face.

Grandpa's hand reached across the room and snapped at Claire and Andrew and Griffin, and those dreaded words were spoken: "THE CLAW! THE CLAW!"

Immediately, three more voices shouted, "THE CLAW! THE CLAW! THE CLAW!" The children were bouncing up and down on the bed, and six little hands were held up in the air, all snapping back at Grandpa.

Grandma was *not* amused.

"Oh, for Pete's sake," said Grandma. "You will never get to sleep making that noise. It is time for all claws, big and little, to go back in their cages. Now *go to sleep!*"

Grandma looked at Grandpa and gave him "*the look*." All was quiet.

"What now?!" thought Grandma, as that mischievous grin crossed Grandpa's face *again*. "Howwwwwwwwwwwl!"

The room immediately filled with coyote howls from Grandpa and the pack of three.

Grandma was *not* amused. She was at her wit's end.

"It is time to sleep," a very exasperated Grandma exclaimed. "No more snoring or tooting or clawing or howling. Close your eyes and *go to sleep*. Good night!"

Grandma looked at Grandpa and gave him *"the look."*

But Grandma was outnumbered. Not one but four very mischievous faces were grinning back at her. Grandpa snored, Griffin tooted, Claire did the claw, and Andrew howled. The children were way too hyper to go to sleep.

Grandma looked at Grandpa to give him *"the look"* but Grandpa had suddenly become very quiet. There was no mischievous grin on his face. He had fallen fast asleep.

An hour later, the tooting, the clawing, and the howling had stopped. The children were finally asleep, but Grandma was not.

When morning arrived, everyone but Grandma bounced out of bed.

"The kids are hungry," Grandpa informed Grandma.

A mischievous grin crossed Grandma's face.

"I think Grandpa would *love* to make the children breakfast," was her reply.

Grandpa looked at Grandma and gave her *"the look."* But Grandma only smiled.

"Call me when the food is ready," she said as she snuggled down in her bed. "My sleepover is not quite over."

After bidding farewell to the children that weekend, a realization dawned on me, my work was not yet done. Because the grandkids were so young, chances were, in the future, they wouldn't remember this wonderful time we had together, and I wanted them to recall every single detail. So driven by this sentiment, I sat down at the kitchen table, pen in hand, and wrote this story, **"The Sleepover."** I'm so glad I made the decision to capture these moments in words. It's a little bit of my grandchildren's history.

Are We Having Fun Yet?

"I think Grandma has really lost it," was the comment I overheard a bewildered Andrew state to his sister and cousins.

The four grandkids were huddled together, discussing their upcoming holiday with Chuck and me, and they had serious doubts about my proposed itinerary. You see, in the past, as the grandkids entered the preteen stage of life, our summer escapades evolved into more than mere vacations—they transformed into week-long travels, whisking us away on trains, planes, buses, and automobiles. These urban ventures unfurled like scrolls of luxury, transporting us into the realm of new experiences, sights, and indulgences that delighted both the young and the young at heart. And now, Grandma was suggesting *this*!

I must admit I was making a drastic change from our past holidays, but a subtle notion had taken root in my mind, sprouting into a compelling plan. It struck me that our holidays should not just include urban explorations but should also encompass the raw thrill of rustic rural adventures with nature as the host. And so, with an idea as simple as it was full of promise, I embarked on a mission to transplant our little city dwellers into the heart of the countryside. The concept was straightforward: we were going to camp beneath the stars.

As I excitedly revealed the upcoming holiday agenda to the group of four, I was met with absolutely no spark of enthusiasm. In fact, a palpable air of indifference hung all around them. However, I was not fazed by their apparent lack of eagerness. After all, they were dealing with a grandma who had taught eight year olds many years before, and she had learned a trick or two from that experience. I would soon have this tough audience eating out of my hand. Armed with a strategy and a lot of determination, I went into full animation mode.

Taking an exaggerated breath, from my toes to my nose, I excitedly exclaimed, "Smell that good old country air."

Grandma is weird, was the expression on their faces.

"Listen to the crickets chirp in the distance," I urged, as I tried unsuccessfully to imitate the sound.

Slight grins and shaking of heads were their response to this.

"We may even see the sunset. Don't you want to stay up late for that?" I asked in an incredulous tone.

However, it seemed, my pleasure-packed visions were not shared.

"This will be fun," I insisted.

But as any seasoned adult might know, uttering those words often precedes an adventure that's anything but. Little did I suspect this attempt to kindle their enthusiasm would be but the prologue to a tale they'd carry with them for a lifetime.

The day arrived. The sky was blue, no signs of rain, a beautiful warm day with a gentle breeze blowing, and miraculously, no bugs nor mosquitoes were in sight. What more could one ask for? It was the perfect weather for camping. I could feel the excitement just welling up inside me. This was it. Another adventure with the grandkids. To set the stage, and to put everyone in the mood, we first watched the classic movie *The Great Outdoors* with John Candy. I love that movie. Lack of interest for my big camping event was still definitely evident, but there were no objections because that is what you do when you love your grandma. You humour the old dear.

The tent was located and dragged out of storage. Chuck and the boys assembled it just steps from the patio door, ensuring nighttime bathroom runs would not be an unwanted adventure. Supper, a true pioneer's feast of hotdogs and more hotdogs, was served on the picnic table, and the smell of marshmallows toasting in the wood-burning potbelly stove filled the air. I think the fancy name is Chiminea, but I'm not fancy, so the description *outside old wood-burning potbelly stove* will do nicely. Smores were messily made. Eventually, it was time to turn in for the night. At that point, I was met by a barrage of questions.

"Are we going to sleep on the ground?" was the first question which was asked in disbelief.

"Well, yes," was my reply.

"Won't that be kind of hard?" was the next inquiry.

Now, this is being said to a seventy-plus-year-old woman with back issues who was ready to sleep on a bed of nails if it would give these kids this wonderful experience.

"Well, what do you have in mind?" I asked, suspecting that these kids probably had a solution to this hardship.

"We could take some cushions off the couch," came the response.

Permission was granted, and I thought my back just might make it through the night after all. The four of them got to work making their nest comfortable while I hunted up pillows and blankets.

"Hope the coyotes don't attack us during the night," Chuck said as he innocently headed towards the tent.

God, there are times I could strangle that man.

After giving Chuck *the look*, I tried to reassure four extremely nervous kids that although they had heard these animals howling like mad the night before, they were very, very far away and wouldn't come this close to the house. Good Lord, if the tent was any closer, it would be in the family room!

As I entered the evening's accommodations, I was immediately struck with the thought that I had been transported to another time and location. A Sultan's tent in the desert came to mind. Cushions from every couch and armchair in the house were spread on the ground. No worry about *The Princess and the Pea* story here. There could be a bed of broken glass under these cushions and one wouldn't feel a thing.

The next issue was to decide who would sleep where. Apparently, Griffin's feet were smelly, Andrew was tooting a lot, and Grandpa was poking everyone. Claire and Mackenna were disgusted! Solution—I would sleep in the middle, with girls on one side of me and the annoying guys on the other.

Everyone was more or less settled when it was suggested ghost stories should be told. A rather weak attempt was made by the children. Grandpa *did not* participate in this activity. He was under strict instructions from me to refrain from sharing any paranormal tales he might have. This piece of advice was also accompanied by *the look*.

Finally, after an eternity passed, everyone fell asleep, with Grandma being the last of the group to reach that state. At 3:01 a.m., there were screams in the tent from all the kids. They were getting wet, which was strange as it wasn't raining. Then it dawned on me. I had forgotten to turn the sprinkler system off, and it automatically came on at 3:00 a.m. Unfortunately, the tent was just a screen one, so the water sprayed directly into one side and went straight out the other side. Our tent had been transformed into a watery sieve. The kids went running into the house, leaving Chuck and I getting wetter by the minute as we hauled in bedding and all those big, heavy cushions. For days, those water-soaked items were propped up along the hall wall in an attempt to dry them out; a true testament to our misadventure.

I know I did not successfully instill in my grandkids a love for camping, but at least they have, more or less, had the experience. But on the other hand, look at the memories that were created, even if they're a little soggy. You can't beat that.

No Plans Are the Best Plans

A nagging worry clouded my thoughts, and panic was setting in: the grandkids were coming for an entire weekend visit, and I wasn't prepared. In the past, being a very organized person, nothing was left to chance. A full itinerary of events and activities was always planned way in advance, but this year, my creative reservoir seemed dry. I was getting myself into a tizzy. What could we do with teenagers that would be fun, full of new experiences, plus worthy of creating great memories?

In a moment of desperation, I turned to Chuck for guidance.

"What should we do with the kids this weekend?" I implored.

Not bothering to even look up from the paper, he replied, "Oh, I don't know, but you will come up with something. You always do."

And with this profound statement, he continued on with his reading, wiping out any stress or responsibility he obviously never felt in the first place. The ball was in my court.

The weekend arrived, along with four excited grandkids.

"What's the plan, Grandma?" they eagerly asked.

Well, I didn't have a plan, but an idea suddenly popped into my head. Knowing kids are very creative, plus wanting to look like their grandma was on top of the situation, I turned the question back on them and asked, "What would you guys like to do?"

And with that question, my brainstorming ended and theirs began.

"We could make supper," suggested Mackenna.

This idea ignited like wildfire.

"I'll do a pasta dish," continued Mackenna.

"I'll work the barbeque," Griffin added.

"I'll do desserts," chimed in Claire.

"I'll do nothing," reported Andrew, who had absolutely no interest in culinary work.

"Andrew will be our go-for-things helper," Claire stated, in a very sisterly, matter-of-fact voice.

That just left Grandma to be convinced.

"We'll all pitch in. It will be fun, Grandma," Mackenna assured me.

The idea of entrusting their young hearts' desires to the kitchen was a bold one, but it resonated with an unexpected charm. These youthful foodies had always held an inexplicable fascination with culinary creations; a passion I had never fully understood. Believe it or not, from the time they were kindergarten age, if they had the choice of watching cartoons on TV or the Food Network, the latter was always the winner. Weird, but true.

So, I thought, *Why not embrace this proposition? They aren't little kids anymore, so let them loose in my kitchen.* Perhaps it was time for Grandma to indulge in a mini-vacation. After all, a pinch of experimentation and a dash of adventure were essential ingredients of any memorable family gathering.

And so, it was. Griffin assumed his mantle as the master of the barbecue with an air of newfound responsibility. Mackenna, with recipe books strewn across the kitchen table and a determined glint in her eye, threw herself into her role as the main course maestro. Claire was beating the daylights out of the eggs, melting butter, and filling up muffin tins at lightning speed. Amidst the culinary frenzy, Andrew, the team's unsung hero, ensured that the creative chaos remained grounded and focused. The kitchen, once a realm dominated by adults, was now alive with the laughter and chatter of these young chefs-in-the-making. Being a wise grandmother, I stayed well out of their way.

With a successful and delicious meal under our belts, this culinary concept begged for expansion. A lunch of weird yet tasty sandwiches was proposed—a taste-testing fiesta, with each of us contributing quirky ingredients. The rules were simple: nothing ridiculous, no extravagance, just the wonderfully unusual. I gave them examples from my childhood—cheese and onion sandwiches, brown sugar delights, and peanut butter and banana concoctions. The challenge—choose sandwich ingredients, prepare a creation, and share it with the group—was accepted.

"Put your taste buds in gear and let your imaginations go wild," were my instructions.

Quite unusual combinations of ingredients were conjured up, but the true amusement lay in listening to my four amateur food critics evaluate and dissect each entry. Even my creation, a simple ensemble of white bread, mayo, ham, cheese, and lettuce with slices of fresh pear barely got a passing grade.

Apparently, it lacked imagination and creativity, and, "Grandma, you should have used a more interesting type of bread. White is just so ordinary."

Well, what do I know?! I felt as if my kitchen had been turned into a cooking show studio with four mini-Gordon Ramsays in charge, who had just banished me to hell.

Other entries received comments such as "a touch too salty, but it brings out the flavour," to "leaves a lingering aftertaste," and "a tad overly sweet."

What an eye-opener it was as I watched these youngsters educate me on the latest trends in cuisine. It certainly was entertaining.

In the blink of an eye, our weekend was over. Amidst board games, swimming, movies, and culinary antics, the hours had slipped away. As sixteen-year-old Claire embraced me in a parting hug, she posed a question that warmed my heart and sealed the success of our endeavour: "Grandma, can we make it two weekends next year?"

The Price of a Cup of Tea

The other day I found myself in the midst of a gathering, surrounded by folks mostly in the forty-to-fifty age bracket. As I mingled from group to group, I couldn't help but eavesdrop on their conversations. At first, I was amused by their banter, but as time went on, I found myself being downright annoyed by their incessant whining and griping. The hot topic du jour? The apparent stress of raising kids in today's world.

Now, these were the very same adults I remembered from their teenage years. Did they conveniently forget the chaos they caused back then? Did they think their own upbringing was a walk in the park for their poor parents? But alas, not a word escaped my lips. They weren't interested in reminiscing about the past; their focus remained only on navigating the challenges and difficulties of the present.

I remember thinking, "Thank God, my own kids aren't like this. They remember the struggles Chuck and I had with their upbringing and harboured no illusions of its simplicity. They understand the reality of raising teenagers."

Then, one afternoon, Steven arrived for a *chat*. The moment he stepped through the door, I could see he had something on his mind.

"Mom," he lamented, "the price of car insurance to cover young drivers is exorbitant. I mean, really, what do insurance companies expect? How can families afford to pay this?"

And before I could give any gems of wisdom regarding this matter, he carried on.

"Claire is going to university in the fall, and she will need a dependable car to get there and back. That's another cost."

And then his next statement blew me away.

"You and Dad had it so much easier when Tammy and I learned to drive."

I couldn't believe what I was hearing. And they talk about the loss of memory we seniors have!

"Son," I calmly and with great control, said, "let me make you a cup of tea, and then we will talk about this."

As he sipped on his drink, I thought, "Ah, karma."

I leaned back in my chair, feet propped on the footstool, and gave him a long, hard look. I could see the more comfortable I was getting, the less comfortable he felt.

I began, "Fasten your seatbelt, son, and let me take you down the memory lane your dad and I travelled with you and Tammy when you first began to drive."

I could sense he was already regretting bringing up this topic for discussion, but he was a captive audience—he hadn't finished his tea.

"Steven," I said, "you both learned to drive and I survived. It may have been hair-raising at times, but I wouldn't have wanted to miss the ride. So, to address your concerns, let me tell you a story. For very good reasons, I think I'll call it Driving Miss Lynda Crazy."

An uneasy look crossed his face as I began my tale.

"Let's begin with Tammy. Your dad's driving skills didn't always follow the code of safe driving, and I knew my nerves couldn't make it through the learning process, so it was agreed that we would enrol her in the Drivers Ed program. Your sister went through the course with no hitches and passed her test. Two years later, when she was heading off to university, we had no worries about buying her a small, second-hand car. We were pretty confident about her driving skills.

"And then it was your turn—and dear Steven, you were certainly a different breed. The Driver's Handbook, which you picked up far in advance of this momentous occasion, was studied extensively. I, too, benefited from this wealth of knowledge . . . well, sort of. I had always thought I was a fairly competent driver, but according to the Driver's Bible, I was not. Seated in the front passenger seat, you became a talking driving instructor, a regular little podcaster.

"'Mom, you didn't signal soon enough. Mom, you're too close to that car. Mom, you stopped too far back from the corner. Mom, why are you so agitated?' and on and on you went.

"Good Lord, you were driving Miss Lynda crazy.

"Before I knew it or wanted it, that little piece of paper was tucked into your wallet and you were a certified driver. It was amazing the amount of driving errands you volunteered to do for me. But now the tables were turned. I was the passenger; and not a very relaxed one, either.

"The floorboards directly in front of me became pretty much worn down, as my foot would hit the imaginary brake whenever I felt you needed to slow down.

"Remember my famous instruction, 'Now there is a stop sign ahead, so stooooooooop.' And I'm sure you haven't forgotten my favourite piece of advice, 'Think of all the other drivers on the road as idiots. Be constantly on the alert for mistakes they might make.'

"Then came the inevitable showdown over the choice of wheels. While Dad advocated for practicality and reliability, you had grand visions of cruising the streets in a *sporty babe-mobile*, whatever that meant. This type of car was not in our budget. Arguments, or perhaps a nicer way of putting it, negotiations, ensued for several days.

"'Do you think we're made of money?' your father demanded. 'Do you have any idea how much the insurance will be for that type of vehicle? Furthermore, you think it will be a babe magnet. I'm telling you; it will be a cop magnet.'

"'But Dad, I don't want an old lady's car like Tammy's,' was your response. 'I've been saving my money for a car since I was thirteen. I can pay the difference between your idea of a dependable vehicle and my vision of a flashy beauty.'

"On those terms, a compromise was reached. You were considerably poorer, but you did get your Toyota Supra.

"So, Steven," I concluded with an air of understanding and *some* compassion, "you be the judge. Has anything really changed over the years regarding teenagers and driving?"

As he left, I hoped he was thinking, "Mom is right. The more things change, the more they stay the same. Mom and Dad can totally relate to what I'm going through."

But I strongly suspect that the thought that was *really* going through his mind was: "Don't accept a cup of tea from Mom."

The Unexpected Request

The doorbell rang. "Who could that be?" I thought, as I made my way to the front entrance. There stood my granddaughter, Claire.

"Just came for a visit, Grandma," she said.

Claire often dropped by unannounced, so I thought nothing about her unexpected appearance. But this was no ordinary visit. Unbeknownst to me, Claire was on a mission.

"So glad to see you, Claire. Come on in." I said, "I'll put the kettle on, and then we can have a good old chat."

As we cradled our cups, our dialogue began. I treasure these moments with Claire. Just listening to what teenagers think and do is such a learning experience for me. It gives me the opportunity to see life through the eyes of the young.

"What's new with you?" I asked her. "How is school going?"

She filled me in on her courses, her friends, and then she said, "My English teacher has given our class an assignment, and it is worth 10 percent of our final grade. We have three weeks to complete it, so I want to get started on it as soon as possible."

"Well, Claire, you were never one to procrastinate. What is this project?" I asked.

Claire took a deep breath, "We are to choose a person we see as a role model and explain why we feel this way. We can either interview someone we know, or we can do research on a person who is famous, living or deceased. Using this material about their lives, we are to write an article which might appear in a newspaper."

"So, let me get this straight. You're pretending to be a journalist or a newspaper reporter, and you need to interview someone you really admire or have admired in history?" I asked.

"That's right," was her reply.

"Well, who is your person?"

Again, there was a moment of hesitation as Claire took another deep breath, "Well Grandma," she said, "I was wondering if I could interview *you?*"

I was at a loss for words. I was definitely surprised and shocked by this request. Imagine, Claire thinking I'm a role model. Good God, she *admires* me. All the crazy, dumb things I had done in my life flashed before my eyes. I felt honoured, but also very nervous. What type of questions were on this agenda? Could I possibly live up to this pedestal she had put me on? I didn't want to blow it for the kid.

"Claire," I said, "I'm not famous, and I'm certainly not dead yet. Are you going to write my future obituary?"

"No, Grandma," she stated emphatically, "be serious."

I could see that since 10 percent of her English grade was riding on this essay, I had better smarten up.

"Okay," I said. "How do we go about this interview, Miss Oprah?"

"Well, I have a list of suggested questions," was her answer.

And so, she began.

"Grandma, as a child, what did you want to be when you grew up?"

"Taller," I said.

I wasn't aware that Claire knew how to give *the look* until that moment. I got her message, loud and clear.

"Okay, Claire, I wanted to be a criminal lawyer. Not the one who would stand up in the courtroom and argue the case before the judge, but the person who did the research, the investigating, the behind-the-scenes work."

Back in the day, I had pictured myself as a member of Perry Mason's team, but no sense telling her that—she would have absolutely no idea who I was referring to. She did, however, understand my *Law & Order* reference.

The next question was posed, "Why did you not follow this dream?"

Hmm, that's a very good question. I was starting to think that maybe I wasn't the great role model Claire thought I was. I didn't want her to think I gave up on my dreams, as that certainly wasn't true. I simply chose other options that would lead to a fulfilling, happy life. And so I explained to her how it was back in the mid-1960s.

"Most girls married a year or two after graduating from high school, so being a stay-at-home wife and mother was often their only choice. University was expensive and a dream for only those who had financial resources. For the rest of us girls who wished to pursue post-secondary education, the career options were limited—a nurse, a teacher, or a secretary. I knew I would enjoy working with young children, so I chose a teaching career."

"Tell me about your teaching days," was the next topic for discussion.

A smile crossed my face as I remembered those little eight-and nine-year-old pupils in my classes. Some names and faces stood out more in my memory than others. I wondered what Julie was doing with her life now, and just last year I ran into Ian, who proudly informed me he was a grandpa. And then, of course, there was the wig episode with Brent. Did he still remember the day he scalped Mrs. Pilon? Oh, the stories I could tell. But Claire wasn't writing a novel, she needed short, concise material for her article, and so I summarized.

"For eight years, I enjoyed teaching grades two and three. I stopped this career when your Aunt Tammy was born, and I was lucky enough to be a stay-at-home mom until your dad started junior kindergarten six years later. However, during this *home* time, I did not abandon my teaching skills. I tutored children from grades three to nine in math."

"When did you get your university degree?"

"Ah, that was a challenge," I said.

Scenes from the past flooded my mind as I saw myself waddling out the door on Saturday mornings since I was pregnant with Steven. Added to this picture was one-and-a-half-year-old Tammy screaming and clinging to my leg trying to prevent me from leaving. I described these happenings to Claire.

"It was as much work getting out the door as it was to do the school assignments," I said, "but getting a university education was a goal I had set for myself, and over time, I did it. One of my proudest moments was making the Dean's honour role. Caring for two little children, tutoring, and getting my university degree with distinction were all amazing accomplishments for me."

"Grandma, you always say your motto is, 'If it's meant to be, it's up to me.' I guess you proved your point there."

I nodded. Nothing was lost on this kid.

"Did you go back to teaching?"

This girl was being thorough with her questions. No stone was being left unturned, and although I knew Claire was familiar with this part of our family history, for the sake of the interview, I gave my answer.

"No. The company Grandpa started when we first got married was expanding, and he needed help running it. We made a great team, your grandpa and I. Grandpa had more time to oversee the men and the jobs while I managed the business and financial aspects of the company. I loved working in the business field, and although Grandpa retired at age sixty-four, I kept on working—although I cut back considerably on my hours—until COVID finally kicked me out the door. I was seventy-three years old at the time."

"When and why did you start your writing career?"

Ah, this was an easy one to answer.

"Being forced into retirement and finding myself in isolation due to COVID restrictions, I knew I would go crazy if I didn't have something to do with my time. I needed a reason to get out of bed in the mornings. I had written a story about you, Griffin, and Andrew years ago, and I thought I would haul it out of storage and perhaps publish it. Now, I had no idea how to go about doing this, but as you have pointed out, I strongly believe in my motto, so I watched webinars, talked to other authors, did my research, and in June 2021, my children's book, *The Sleepover*, launched on Amazon. Who would have thought your grandma would start a new career in her seventies?"

"Are you continuing this career?"

"Yes. The writing bug has bitten me. Furthermore, I have a constant source of writing material—just look at the weird and wonderful things our family does."

"I'm, not sure Grandpa is happy being a *source*," laughed Claire.

"Grandpa doesn't mind," I assured her, "he's a pretty good sport. Plus, what can he say? The stories are true. He can't deny that."

I continued, "I also started a bi-weekly blog I called *From the Senior's Corner* around the time I published my book, and a year later, I started a newsletter, *That's All She Wrote*. And here I am, at the ripe old age of seventy-seven, publishing my second book, *We May Not Be Crazy, But Sometimes I Wonder*. Claire, I think the Pilon family is living proof of that saying."

"What are your plans for the future?"

I wanted to say, "To breathe as long as possible," but I didn't dare voice that thought. Instead, I answered sincerely, "Well, I have considered retiring when I turn eighty, but I'm sure something will come along at that time to grab my interest, so retirement will probably be postponed once again."

"Well," I thought, "we have more or less covered my life story. This interview must be almost over."

But Claire was not quite done. There was one last question.

"Grandma, what is your philosophy on life?"

Good God, did she really ask me that question?

Because Claire could read my mind, she hastily added, "No silly response, Grandma. I need a good answer."

How could I possibly sum up seventy-seven years of living in just a few words? I paused, giving this question a great deal of thought before I answered.

"Well, Claire, successes undoubtedly bring joy and fulfillment, but failures hold an equal significance in life's journey. Through my experiences, I've come to appreciate that making mistakes can be a blessing in disguise. They serve as invaluable opportunities for learning, growth, and self-discovery. Each failure offers a second chance; a renewed opportunity to approach challenges with wisdom and determination, ultimately leading to a more fulfilling path forward. So, Claire, never give up on your dreams. Life is what you make it. Remember my motto: 'If it's meant to be, it's up to me.'"

The interview was finished. Whew! Claire was happy and I was relieved. I felt we had done our best towards achieving that full 10 percent grade. I never asked to read her final report. The fact I was invited to participate in this endeavour was enough for me. My heart was full.

CHAPTER 2

TALES OF SLEEP DEPRIVATION

Sleep? What is that? Is it something you eat?
L. Pilon

Parent Trickery

I've always hated seeing toddlers walking around with pacifiers stuck in their mouths. It just looks so ridiculous. What's wrong with their parents? Don't they realize these things might affect the development of the child's teeth, maybe even hinder his speech progress? When I see a two or three year old chomping on a soother, it's all I can do not to yank the darn thing out of his mouth.

"No kid of mine is ever going to have one," I vowed.

These were my strong views and beliefs during my *pre-kid* stage of life.

And then along came parenthood. The arrival of one's firstborn brings so much joy, so much excitement, and so much exhaustion— you will never, ever have a decent night's sleep again. My journey into the realm of parental sleep deprivation has been nothing short of a wild rollercoaster ride, complete with unexpected twists and turns. The minute we brought her home from the hospital, Tammy, this tiny terror, this little forty-winks saboteur, declared war on my precious slumber. I was becoming a bleary-eyed zombie. Something had to be done. Have you ever heard of The Mother of the Year award? Well, just let me state, I didn't even come close to achieving that honour, but I did come up with an ingenious, albeit slightly unorthodox, plan to reclaim my sleep.

The strategy began the day I complained to my friend, Judy. "I don't know how I can survive," I sighed. "Tammy treats the night like a buffet of mini-naps. I'm so tired all the time."

"Get the kid a soother," this mother of three instructed, in a matter-of-fact tone. "That will work."

As a new parent, I was starting to realize that perhaps childless couples don't always deal with reality. Maybe it was time I took advice from someone who was actually in the trenches.

A trip to Walmart procured the suggested item. Now, I still harboured a distaste for the use of a soother, so I struck a compromise with myself—no soother during Tammy's waking hours, but come nighttime, well, that was a different story altogether. The moment bedtime approached, that pacifier found its place in Tammy's mouth. Boy, did our little girl love her soother; it was her ticket to dreamland, whisking her off to sleep in no time. But this plugged-in solution was only partially successful. During the early hours of the morning, the soother would go MIA and then all hell would break loose. Relentless crying would continue until I crawled out of bed, located it, and stuck the blessed thing back into her mouth, where she would happily clamp down on it, only to lose it again a few minutes later. This routine, which carried on for months, occurred two or more times a night, and I was beat. It always amazed me how Chuck could sleep peacefully through all this howling. With the arrival of our second child only a few weeks away, I knew I had to take action. No way would this sleep-deprived body be able to look after two little ones. And then I had a light bulb moment. I had an idea.

My method of fixing this problem would certainly be frowned upon today, but it was 1975, and the universe was a little more sympathetic towards the actions of parents. I realized it was time to wean Tammy off the soother, as in my view, she was too old for one.

"How would I break her of the pacifier habit?" one might ask.

Well, not to worry, my mind had been working overtime. I had the answer. I took her soother and, using a pair of scissors, I put a tiny cut in the end of it. Now, when Tammy put it in her mouth, it would pinch, just a little. It was no longer the pleasurable device she was familiar with.

"This bad soother is broken," I sadly told her. "It might hurt Tammy, so we better get rid of it."

I had visions of her searching our house high and low for this cherished object, so together we placed it in the kitchen garbage can. However, the problem, unlike the soother, did not disappear immediately. For a few nights, Tammy fussed and cried, but I knew there was nothing wrong with her. She just needed to get used to life as a big girl.

"How will I ever live through these nights of unnecessary crying?" I thought.

And then, like a bolt of lightning from the sky, inspiration hit me. I had tricked our daughter into a new routine, now it was time for me to trick my own mind into a different course of action.

"Lynda, pretend you are a man. Men don't hear crying children during the night," I thought.

And it worked! Things changed when I realized this little girl was manipulating me. For the next week, I was a *man* in my mind, and then, lo and behold, the middle-of-the-night crying stopped. Restful snores, rather than restless struggles, were mine. Ah, nirvana at last. My unconventional actions and techniques may not meet with the approval of the child experts of today, but I don't care. I never slept better.

Footnote: Steven, our second child, never had a soother.

Hot Babes

"Get a good night's sleep, and you'll feel better."

Great advice! Now, if only someone could explain to me what this *sleep* thing actually is. As women, we embark on a lifelong quest through the stages of infancy and child-rearing, all in pursuit of this mythical creature called sleep. And through it all, we are tired, tired, tired. Then, just when we think that glorious uninterrupted sleep is within our grasp, BAM! Hormonal factors kick into full gear. Do women ever catch a break? This search for peaceful slumber was no simple matter. I wondered how I would cope.

Well, just ask the men in my life, and they will tell you, "Mom didn't cope, we had to."

Ah, the hardships men have to endure!

Menopause, the stage that gives every woman not only a smoking hot body, but also the gift of insomnia, was knocking at my door. Every morning I would drag myself out of bed feeling cranky, tired, and lethargic. Tammy didn't fall victim to these bad, irritable moods, as she was away at university, but Chuck and Steven were not so lucky. Walking into the kitchen and seeing two happy guys sitting there eating breakfast could set me off. You see, it didn't take much for me to lose it. Just a sideways glance or a laugh from them when I felt so miserable could do the trick. I swear, I could chew them up and spit them out long before they finished breakfast. It was amazing how fast the two of them could clear out of the house. When normal sleep patterns eventually returned, so did the good-natured old mom, thank God, because even I didn't like the monster version of her.

During this *change of life* (honest to God, a man must have coined that ridiculous phrase), a woman's internal thermostat oscillates between warmth and chilliness, resembling the wagging tail of an excited puppy. Chuck's body temperature seems to stay relatively the same winter or summer. He is like Goldilocks, who has found Little Bear's bed. Temperature-wise, everything is just right. He falls asleep the instant his head hits the pillow, and rarely does he move from this initial position of sleeping bliss. Covers stay in place, as does his body. He just doesn't move. I, on the other hand, can flail around all night with covers on, covers off—repeat. I can freeze and overheat, all in the blink of an eye. The fan gets no rest. It goes full blast in the summer and in the dead of winter, along with the *one-leg-out-of-the-covers* technique to deal with these nightly sweats. I am prepared for all conditions. A stack of blankets is readily available at the foot of my bed because I know the next cold front will be fast approaching.

Although women have become very creative in implementing our own heating and cooling devices, good quality sleep often eludes us. I had tried to solve or at least live through the biological causes and the gender-based expectations that had contributed to my sleep issues, but I wasn't done yet. There was still one avenue left to explore. I would check out my environment and make the necessary changes and improvements so that sleep would welcome me with open arms. My mission was to wake up refreshed, regenerated, and ready to face the day with all its challenges. I would not give up on my search. There had to be a way to accomplish this blessed state. Slowly, the seed of an idea began to germinate, quietly taking root in my mind. Action needed to be taken, and I was ready.

It's All in The Bed

No matter how I arranged the pillows around and under my body, an undisturbed night's sleep was still an impossible dream. I would wake up in the morning having endured a restless night, which resulted in backaches and pains. Chuck, however, has never had any sleep issues. I'm convinced that guy can sleep standing up. Over the years, we experimented with different styles of mattresses with varying support systems, but nothing worked for me. Finally, I could not take it any longer. Enough was enough. Something had to be done. Maybe it was time to check out adjustable beds.

We made a trip to the Sleep Country store, where we were greeted by a very pleasant lady named Susan, who had obviously not reached her sales quota for the week. We explained our situation to her, and she immediately escorted us to the electric bed section. Twenty years ago, there wasn't a large selection, or at least in this store that was the case. There were three options: a queen size bed with one remote, a queen size bed split in the middle with two remotes, or the last choice, twin beds each with its own control. Well, it was a no-brainer. Twin beds it was.

Because these beds required special mattresses, again there was a limited choice, which was actually a good thing. Susan suggested we lie on each mattress and see which one was the most comfortable for us, plus it would also give us a chance to experiment with the remote and try out the different positions. Good Lord, the remote even had a massage button. I could see I was losing Chuck. There was no darn way he was going to lie down on a bed in a busy store, pushing a bunch of buttons, vibrating, and looking like an idiot. I secretly agreed with him, but I dutifully laid down on each mattress for approximately two minutes, which seemed like an eternity. But really, how could one accurately assess how comfortable a mattress was under these conditions? Since they had a thirty day return policy, we decided to take a chance on the Sealy Pocket Coil Comfort Silk Pillowtop. At least the name sounded comfortable. The purchases were made, a delivery date was decided on, and two very confused people left the store wondering what on Earth they had just bought. A smiling Susan had reached her sales quota for the week.

The beds arrived, were assembled, and then it was time to set them to the most comfortable positions for each of us.

Following a couple of half-hearted attempts at this task, Chuck impatiently announced, "I'm quite comfortable sleeping flat. I'm not going to be pushing any stupid buttons."

I thought, "Well, the purchasing of his bed was rather a waste of money."

After a few days of experimenting, I discovered the perfect sleep position for me. My sweet spot was in the shape of a V with my head elevated, my bum dropping into the hollow and my knees in a slanted elevated position. The remote allowed me to lock into this exact position so with a single push of a button the mattress would shift immediately into it.

A few nights later, Chuck went up to bed while I did the woman's nightly checklist—lock the doors, turn off all the lights, check if the stove is turned off, oh wait, did I check the back door? Naturally, Chuck was sound asleep by the time I got upstairs. I grabbed the remote and, facing my bed, I pushed the automatic position button. Nothing happened. I pushed the button again. The mattress did not move. The green light on the remote winked back at me, so obviously the batteries were working. This time I pushed several *new* buttons.

All of a sudden, from behind me came this very loud, ticked-off voice, "What the hell are you doing?"

I turned around and there was Chuck all scrunched up with his knees touching his chin. I had grabbed *his* remote. Unable to contain myself, I burst into laughter, tears streaming down my face. Trust me, my reaction did absolutely nothing to improve his mood. That night, sleep evaded me once again, but for an entirely different reason. I could not stop laughing as the comical image of Chuck persisted in my mind.

Chuck's frustration with the adjustable bed situation, and his annoyance with me, lingered for a few days, but eventually he was able to see the funny side of the situation. Our adjustable beds, originally purchased for a restful night's sleep, unexpectedly delivered an added dimension of comfort: the joy of shared laughter and a great story to tell our kids.

The Calm Before the Horn

Over the years, life has taught me that the best-laid plans often take unexpected turns. What initially appears as a tranquil, straightforward endeavour can swiftly transform into a heart-pounding adventure full of surprises and adrenaline-fuelled moments. A few days ago, a memory of such an experience came floating back to me.

I was playing a card game on my iPad, telling myself I wasn't wasting time but rather participating in an exercise to aid my memory and to increase my brain power, when an advertisement for an app called Calm popped up. Now, normally I hit the X in the far-right corner of the screen and carry on with my game, but this particular promotion grabbed my attention.

"Calm is the app for sleep, meditation, and relaxation. It will help you manage stress, balance moods, sleep better, and refocus your attention," the announcement boasted.

This software contained sounds for rain and thunderstorms, for oceans and rivers, for crickets and frogs, for wind, fire, birds, and the list went on and on. Plus, within each of these categories were subcategories.

My mind instantly went back in time, long before CDs or apps were even invented, to the days when you were really techie if you owned and knew how to operate the little cassette tape recorder. In the late 1980s, Chuck and I practised unwinding at the end of our day and getting a good night's sleep by listening to the sounds of nature captured on these little tapes. At that time, one could purchase recordings of various sounds such as babbling brooks, thunderstorms, ocean waves, and rain. Gift shops and other trendy little boutiques often had a circuit board located right beside these items, so with a push of a button, you could hear small segments of each cassette. This was a great help in deciding which one was the proper fit to serve your needs. It was quite leading-edge technology back in the day. Over the months, I had added to our collection, but apparently, we were missing one of nature's greatest gifts: the wind.

"You know," said Chuck, "there is nothing better than walking through the bush on a windy day and listening to the wind moving through the trees. God, I love that sound. What are the chances of getting a cassette of that?"

My mission was assigned. In the following weeks, I searched everywhere imaginable for this requested item, but stores in the nearby towns and cities did not carry this particular sound of nature. The restless, wayward wind could not be found.

After explaining this failure to a very disappointed Chuck, I decided there had to be another option. Why couldn't I make a recording of the wind? For the next few weeks, the city of Brampton experienced a period of rather calm, uneventful weather, but then one evening in October an opportunity presented itself. The wind was howling, and I decided to put my little tape recorder outside for the night to catch this phenomenon. After all, the machine would automatically shut off once the tape was full, so it did not require my attention throughout the recording. Off I went to bed, thinking I had quite nicely solved this problem. We would enjoy the fruits of my labour the next evening.

I could hardly contain my excitement. The following night, as we crawled into bed, I said to Chuck, "Have I got a surprise for you tonight!" (Get your mind out of the gutter, I was referring to the tape!)

We listened to the first few minutes, and it was agreed that, yes, indeed, it was a lovely calming sound. We blissfully drifted off to sleep with the noise of the wind blowing all around us.

I'm not sure how long we slept, but all of a sudden, the air horn of an eighteen-wheeler tractor trailer blasted right in our bedroom. As fast as a speeding bullet, two very wide-eyed people shot upright in bed and beyond. We were convinced we were sleeping in the middle of the 401.

"What on Earth was that?"

After our heads were retrieved from the ceiling, our heart rates slowed down, and our night clothes had been checked to verify no signs of accidents there, we realized that all was well. Apparently, during the night of taping, a transport truck travelling on the nearby highway had decided, for whatever reason, to lay on his horn for all the world to hear.

My wind recording did not manage stress or balance moods, nor did it improve the quality of our sleep, but it certainly got our attention. I'm not sure what happened to that tape, but I do know it had a very short life. It simply blew away that night, never to be listened to again.

CHAPTER 3

THE GOLDEN YEARS

May your golden years be tarnish free.
L. Pilon

Retirement: From City Life to Country Dreams

In the heart of every well-lived life, there comes a time when the curtain falls on the daily grind and a new chapter titled 'Retirement' begins. The prospect gleams with the allure of endless leisure, a departure from the hustle and bustle that defined the years prior. Dreams of morning sleep-ins, exotic trips, and the luxury of unstructured days dance in the minds of those who've toiled for decades. But beware: an unspoken truth often emerges. This coveted transition from work to leisure can hold a surprising emptiness for those unprepared to navigate this vast expanse of free time. Because I was aware of this possibility, I was determined that our golden years would not tarnish under the weight of inactivity. I had a plan.

I found myself pondering Chuck's retirement with a mix of curiosity and concern. This was a man wired for perpetual motion;

an unyielding force of activity. Our little bungalow, which had stood as our haven for over four decades, had been meticulously revamped and modernized to demand minimal upkeep. Only our tiny yard required attention, and let's be frank, cutting a few feet of grass each week was no large undertaking. I knew if I wanted to survive, plus have a harmonious coexistence in this major lifestyle shift, strategic measures had to be orchestrated well in advance. I must admit, my intentions were not entirely altruistic. Although my paramount desire was to witness Chuck enjoying this well-earned stage of life, I must confess to another motive. I aimed to prevent the remote possibility of me committing murder stemming from an excess of our proximity. Tripping over him every time I turned around in my kitchen was not my idea of fun. In my opinion, a husband engaged in purposeful pursuits and interests and in his own space equated to a harmonious household for a wife who sought equilibrium. In the careful choreography of his post-retirement timetable lay the key to my serenity and my sanity.

When we were in our early fifties, Chuck would often say, "When I retire, I'm going to buy one of those big RVs and we can travel around the country and see the sights."

Now, this might have been his idea of fun and adventure at the time, but it certainly wasn't mine.

"Have you looked at the drivers of those big gas guzzling things?" I asked him. "They are at least eighty years old and just waiting to have a heart attack."

To further make my point, I continued on. "Do you know how many five-star hotels you could stay at before you spent anywhere near what the cost of that beast would be, the gas, the insurance, the maintenance, plus it only depreciates over time."

And then, to finalize my argument, "Those things are just housework on wheels for the woman."

We never bought a camper. Now, don't get me wrong. I think this is a great idea for those who love the great outdoors and all the things that go with that type of lifestyle, but it wasn't for us. The fact was, neither Chuck nor I liked camping. I had another idea.

Chuck was not the least bit interested in sports, had only a few male buddies outside of our couple friends, and didn't have many hobbies. What would make him happy? Chuck is a farm boy at heart, so the solution was to buy a few acres in the country, a hobby farm, so he could buy and then play with his Tonka toys—lawn tractors, a wagon, ATVs, plus other machinery he deemed necessary. In 2005, we bought the farm. Chuck was in his glory. He had something to occupy his retirement time. He had a purpose. Now he just had to pick his date for retirement.

I had always pictured Chuck as one of those old codgers leaning on a cane, showing up at work every morning until the day he died. You see, on April 1, 1968, at the age of twenty-two, this farm boy started a window and door business. As the company flourished, I left my teaching career to spearhead the business operations, allowing Chuck the opportunity to focus more on overseeing our expanding projects. Together, we made a great team. As our enterprise continued to grow, our children also became involved, truly solidifying our business as a family affair in every respect.

One Saturday morning when we were having our bi-weekly meeting, I said to the kids, "You know, Dad and I will probably retire when we turn sixty-five."

Chuck looked at me, and in a firm, no-nonsense tone of voice said, "There is no damn way I am going to work until I'm sixty-five."

Now, the fact that Chuck was already sixty-four and that we owned a family business made this news shocking and totally unexpected.

"When do you want to retire, Dad?" asked a somewhat surprised Steven.

"Today," came the reply.

"But you can't retire, today," said Steven. "I have jobs booked for you until Wednesday afternoon."

"Then Wednesday will be my last day," said Chuck.

And so, it was.

You see, Chuck had a new career he couldn't wait to start. The allure of life as a farmer was calling out to him with great enthusiasm. Chuck was on cloud nine. He had his daily job list, which gave him a reason to get up each morning and do the things he *wanted* to do. Furthermore, retirement gave him those extra hours to complete and supervise jobs he had put off in the past. One such job on this new agenda was overseeing the paving of the driveway and parking lot at work. I call this little adventure the Outfoxed by a Groundhog Project.

Our company shop backs onto a ravine where a variety of wildlife resides. The prime reason for this increase in population occurred when Chuck and Steven built a shelter for all the stray cats living in the area. Word soon got out in the neighbourhood that a cozy, heated (yes, I said heated), two story 4' x 4' cat house had opened up; and it also served food once a day, six days a week. You never knew who would show up at the trough—cats, groundhogs, raccoons, or the odd opossum. Everyone got along as they all ate side by side. I'm proud to say this multicultural community exhibited no racism; all were tolerated.

Beside the back steps, a portly groundhog, whom we named Barney, had located the perfect spot for his home. This creature, equipped with digging claws that would put a backhoe to shame, was an undisputed champion of underground real estate development. Unlike today's construction crews, Barney had completed the job in no time. His humble abode, a burrow-bungalow, was ready for occupancy. This lovely piece of real estate was ideal for him, as it was only waddling distance from the daily buffet. Over time, as Barney continued to grow in size, so did the entrance to his home. He had certainly upgraded, but his digging had consequences. This mansion-sized hole was fast becoming a safety issue for anyone using the steps. It was time to repave the parking lot.

We assumed Barney would vacate the premises as soon as he heard all the commotion and noise from the equipment, but if that didn't persuade him to go, surely the strong sulfur-like smell of the hot asphalt being poured would get him moving. Therefore, without any investigation on our part, gravel, crushed stone, and four inches of pavement were poured over his home. Imagine our surprise when, the next morning, we found the burrow had not only reappeared, but also was much larger than it had previously been. And there, just a few steps away, was one very ticked off groundhog. Patches of tar hanging from his fur, and his teeth chattering away at lightning speed, he gave us a piece of his mind before he lumbered off into the ravine. But the fact remained that Barney had to go.

Now, there are two ways to get rid of a groundhog—the humane way and the not so humane way (beat it over the head with a shovel). Chuck, being an animal lover, decided on the former. A trap was set, extra smelly cat food used for bait, and an excited

Chuck waited until the next morning. Victory! The groundhog had been caught. A trip to the country was arranged for Barney, and everyone breathed a sigh of relief. The hole could now be filled. However, a new tenant had apparently subleased the place, as Mama Groundhog was spotted scurrying into the hole. A considerable amount of Chuck's time was now spent on attempting to be a great wildlife hunter. Three raccoons, one possum, and one very irate tom cat, who was the most dangerous of all, were captured, Mama was eventually evicted, and the paving job was finally completed.

And me? I just thanked God I wasn't yet retired with spare time on my hands.

Ma'am Is Not Home

"I'm not listening to a bunch of idiots trying to get money from me," Chuck proclaimed.

And thus, the saga began.

Many of you might recall a bygone era when telephones were firmly attached to walls, their lengthy ten-foot cords granting the luxury of stretching into the adjacent room for a morsel of privacy. In my youth, the resonant chime of a ringing phone would set off a frenzy; a wild dash as everyone vied to seize the receiver in the fervent hope the call was meant for them. Such interactions were rare gems, each one holding significance and treasured deeply. However, the march of time brings with it transformations, and now, the once-piercing ring of the landline phone no longer ignites a scramble but rather elicits a collective sigh of weariness. The art now lies in trying to evade these calls altogether. Who is responsible for rewiring the very essence of phone communications? The answer: telemarketers and swindlers. So, how do we navigate these unwanted calls?

The senior populace, tethered to their abodes more often, bears the distinct honour of facing these charlatans on a near-daily basis. I, for one, had no inkling of the myriad of ducts needing cleaning, the warrants poised for my arrest due to tax delinquency, nor the credit card impostors wreaking havoc with my accounts until these unbidden yet oddly informed voices enlightened me.

Chuck had no patience with these callers. I vetoed a few of his suggestions on how he would handle these guys, there was no need for obscenities, and so it was decided that he would *not* answer these calls. Instead, I would program into the phone the names and numbers of family and friends he knew. When these contacts flashed up on caller ID, he was good to go. As for answering the remaining rings, well, they were all mine; my vexing companions to deal with. And trust me, few things rival the annoyance of a 7:00 a.m. call from a disconcertingly cheery voice chirping, "Good morning, Ma'am. I'm Johnathon."

The moment *ma'am* escaped his lips, Johnathon's ship of interest had already sailed. For me, that term conjures an image of someone considerably older—and who, pray tell, is old around here? Certainly not me! Furthermore, it was 7:00 a.m., for Pete's sake. I hadn't even had my coffee yet.

My journey through interactions with these persistent callers has taken quite a few twists and turns. Back in my younger days, armed with ample patience and my inherent Canadian politeness, I would lend a courteous ear to their spiel. Once they were done, I'd calmly provide my reasons for not being interested and gracefully end the conversation. As time marched on and the frequency of these calls grew, my patience wore thin, and my demeanour shifted. This marked the transition to my next phase.

When the voice on the other end inquired, "How are you feeling today, ma'am?" I adopted a new course of action.

"Ah, I'm so appreciative of your concern," I'd reply, my tone dripping with sarcasm.

Then, I'd dive into an elaborate portrayal of every imaginary ailment and misfortune my mind could conjure. Often, Johnathon, or whatever name was used, would hastily interject with an apologetic tone, before being the first to hang up. However, this tactic required a fair bit of energy, and I began to resent the time these calls were siphoning from my life. Swiftly, I found myself moving onto a different approach.

This period witnessed a subtle evolution in my strategy. Upon picking up the phone and hearing the telltale pause after my greeting, the dead giveaway of a cold call, I would decisively hang up. This was a more efficient way to navigate these encounters, saving both time and sanity.

And now, I find myself at the culminating chapter of my dealings with these pesky people. Before even lifting the receiver, I take a quick glance at the caller ID, adhering to the wisdom of the old adage "If it looks like a duck, swims like a duck, and quacks like a duck, it probably is a duck."

In other words, if it looks like a telemarketer's number, chances are it is a telemarketer's number, so ignore the call. I have, at last, learned how to avoid this annoyance altogether.

And so, in the ever-evolving landscape of communication, I've come to embrace a newfound harmony with the relentless barrage of telemarketing calls. The journey through irritation, sarcasm, and cold detachment has led me to a place of quiet triumph. No longer a pawn in their scripted conversations, I stand as master of my phone line. As the sun sets on another day and the landline phone sits in its place, no longer a source of chaos, I reflect on all the scams they promote, such as the mysterious person who used my credit card at four in the morning on an unspecified item. I hope she is enjoying her purchase.

Your Kids Don't Want Your Junk

A seemingly innocent article, nestled within the pages of the daily newspaper, caught my attention. It stated a truth that had been gathering momentum—Canadians were on the brink of inheriting a staggering one trillion dollars over the next decade. This monumental transfer of wealth promised affluence, but it also bore a more insidious burden: an overabundance of possessions. Houses, investments, bank accounts, these were the expected legacies. But intertwined with these riches were items that carried no weight in currency, yet heavy with sentiment—the trinkets, heirlooms, and keepsakes that had adorned our lives.

The writer's words echoed with stark clarity, "Your kids don't want your junk."

The hairs on the back of my neck immediately went up. I was annoyed. What did he mean, our junk? That so-called *junk* is important to seniors. Memories are attached.

But unfortunately, the writer had a persuasive point. The value we once attached to cut glass bowls, fine china, and cherished mementos has dwindled in the face of a disposable culture. The modern era embraces convenience, leaving no room for the storage of memories in porcelain or crystal. The article implored seniors to unburden themselves of these physical echoes of the past.

Now, I will admit that most seniors are hoarders. We were taught as youngsters that money didn't grow on trees and if you took care of the pennies, the dollars would take care of themselves. Recycling was a way of life long before it became the fashionable thing to do in today's society. There was no waste. For most of the senior population, that saving mentality has stuck with us our entire lives.

Yes, I am guilty of having this perspective. Our home contains a lifetime's worth of accumulation. Each item holds a story, a memory, a piece of my heart. Yet, they are destined to become orphans in a world that no longer holds space for such treasures. A bittersweet ache gripped me, threading through my resolve like ivy around a garden trellis.

Caught between the nostalgia that clung to my belongings and the pragmatic understanding that my children's lives were distinct from mine, I found myself in a precarious dance. It was a delicate waltz between sentiment and practicality, memory and detachment. The concept of decluttering was simple; its execution was anything but. I decided to discuss my dilemma with my children. Maybe they would have some helpful insights on how to accomplish this painful purging job. But alas, they are from a different time, and they couldn't understand my problem.

"If you aren't using it Mom, get rid of it," were the instructions I was given.

"Hmm, good advice," I said, nodding my approval to their words of wisdom.

Immediately, the light went on. Good Lord, Mom was downsizing, decluttering, donating, or whatever one wants to call it, and they wanted no part of it. No way were their homes going to be the new Goodwill drop-off locations. They were now on high alert.

When I asked Tammy, "How full is your china cabinet?"

I couldn't believe how fast she responded with, "Oh Mom, I'm glad you asked. It's overflowing with so much stuff, I thought I would give you a few things from it."

Damn!

And then there is Steven who frisks me every time I enter his home and heaven help me if I'm carrying a box or a bag.

I look at some of my possessions and I say to my kids, "Now don't put that item in a garage sale with a buck-fifty price tag slapped on the side of it. It's worth a lot more than that."

But I don't need to worry about that happening, as no one does estate garage sales any more; too much work sorting and organizing the event. In reality, my prized stuff will ultimately have three destinations—the garbage dumpster, Goodwill, or to a storage unit where it will never see the light of day again unless some guy from *Storage Wars* trips upon it.

Maybe I should make life a little easier for Tammy and Steven and attempt to declutter, pitch, or give away some of my personal items, but I will need two things in order to accomplish this feat: the elusive energy required for such a task and the more elusive "I don't need this crap" attitude. Both, as I have discovered, are harder to summon than anticipated.

The purging is far from over and may never be completed by me. But, on the other hand, I have had a few laughs while attempting to do this job. Every so often, when the kids visit, I get the greatest pleasure in taking them to our basement and garage, both overflowing with our treasures, soon to be their junk, and saying to both of them, "Someday, this will be all yours."

Half the Fun is Getting There

Ah, retirement—that magical time when you trade in your work shoes for flip-flops and your briefcase for a beach bag. Freedom and time were finally ours for the taking. As I stood gazing at the horizon of endless possibilities, I couldn't help but feel a surge of excitement. Chuck and I were gearing up for our first post-retirement trip, a five-day getaway. With the spring in our step somewhat subdued by the weight of wisdom, I knew some adjustments were in order. Our fitness, energy, and stamina levels would need to be factored into our itineraries. Let's face it, we were no longer spring chickens, but we hadn't fallen under the axe yet, either.

With our destination locked in and a direct flight secured, it was time to tackle the dreaded task of packing. Gone were the days of packing for every possible weather scenario or fashion emergency. After all, who wants to lug around excess baggage like a pack mule? Less luggage equalled more freedom—a concept I understood.

"Wouldn't it be great if, in the near future, technology would bless us with clothing that could be shrunk to the size of a pill? Just add water, and voilà! Your outfit springs to life," I thought.

Well, until this sci-fi dream materialized, it was all about streamlined carry-on luggage for us.

Despite my meticulously laid plans—from digitized boarding passes to pre-booked seats—I still couldn't shake off a feeling of uneasiness as we approached the airport. Images of endless queues, flight cancellations, and irritable passengers swirled around in my head. But lo and behold, we arrived early to find no lines in sight and our flight was departing on time. Talk about a retirement bonus! It seemed like we were living the dream. But alas, as is often the case, reality was lurking just around the corner.

Chuck drifted through security like a warm summer breeze, but when I attempted to cross over to the other side, so to speak, all hell broke loose. Alarms beeped. Eyes immediately turned in my direction. Repeated trips walking through the security arch yielded the same results, 'beep, beep.' Did they think I was concealing weapons in my panties? I expected to see a SWAT team arrive at any moment. A female agent, rather large in stature, approached with instructions for me to do the following—feet apart, hands arched over my head. Three times doing this little dance changed nothing. By now, I was beginning to get a little rattled. It was starting to look like this old girl might be considered a security risk. The next step in this humiliating encounter was the need for a *pat down*. Now, I'm all for new experiences, but really, this seemed like taking things a bit too far. Nevertheless, there was no choice, as this no-nonsense guard had already swung into action. Images of drug dealers leaning against a car, being patted down, and then arrested by police flashed through my mind. After two or three *good feels*, I was allowed to move on. No explanation was given for this baffling security incident, and I was just too unravelled to ask.

As I rushed to board the plane before the doors sealed shut, a familiar adage sprang to mind, "Getting there is half the fun."

Really? What idiot said that?!

We reached our destination without any further hiccups. Exploring Quebec City was a wonderful experience, from soaking in the sights to savouring the delicious local cuisine and meeting the wonderfully friendly people. Day five arrived too quickly. It was time to say farewell to this lovely old city.

On this holiday, airport scrutiny was not my friend. Again, on the return journey, Chuck sailed through security in the blink of an eye. When it was my turn to walk through the body scanner, I was not so lucky. The machine, once again, uttered that annoying beep. I was asked to walk through this device several times, but the source of the problem could not be found. I was starting to know the drill. The *wand* was then whipped out, and I was told to stand with my legs spread apart and my arms held out at 180 degrees. This six-foot, two-hundred-pound-plus guard, whom I silently nicknamed Broom-Hilda, loomed over my petite five-foot frame. With an aura of preparation for a formidable battle, she meticulously swept the security wand in every conceivable direction across my body, conducting a screening which, in my estimation, far exceeded the usual routine. However, her efforts yielded no results. I was then ordered to sit in a chair while this thorough wand examination was again performed. No success.

Finally, the exasperated security officer demanded in a voice tinged with frustration and authority, "Have you had any past operations?"

My response, "a titanium hip replacement," set her mind at ease.

I could move on. I can honestly say that on this trip, I was searched from top to bottom and everywhere in between, with no bones left unturned.

Safely back home, Chuck made the comment, "Well, that was an experience and a half. Maybe we should rethink this whole travel idea."

"An excellent suggestion," I replied, "perhaps it is time for us to enter the cruise market for our next trip."

He looked at me as though I had lost my mind.

"There is no way I am going on a cruise," he emphatically informed me. "I don't like the water. I don't like boats. And besides, I can't swim."

That was his argument.

"Well," I replied, "you go on an airplane, and you can't fly."

Silence filled the room.

I love having the last word!

Mind Travel: All Aboard

Planes, trains, and automobiles may whisk us away to far-off destinations, but there's a magic beyond mere transportation in taking a trip—it resides in the power of one's imagination. You see, for me, the fine art of people-watching is my passport to another world, a journey of thoughts and images that unfurl right before my eyes. Nestled amidst the bustling heart of the mall, amid the rush of shoppers scurrying to and fro, I've discovered my own unique means of embarking on this remarkable odyssey. While most individuals pause for a hasty caffeine infusion before retreating to the comforts of home after a long day of retail therapy, I opt for a more unconventional indulgence. I settle my weary old bones onto a timeworn bench, letting my bundles of purchases rest by my feet, and simply observe. As the sea of humanity drifts by, I endeavour to decipher the burdens they carry and the inner musings that accompany their daily routines. In these moments, my imagination truly comes to life, painting vivid stories in my mind.

Take, for instance, that frazzled mother, her patience worn thin by her unruly child throwing a tantrum. I imagine he didn't get the toy he was demanding. I can practically hear her inner monologue, simmering beneath her composed exterior.

"Just you wait until we get home," she silently seethes.

In my day, there was a possibility of two things occurring as a result of this behaviour: the kid would either get sent to a corner for a certain period of time or a hand would lightly cross his butt. But there isn't much chance of these discipline options being chosen. In today's parenting world, a conversation will probably take place between mother and child.

"Now, why do you think Mommy is upset? What do you think your punishment should be?"

The ultimate sentence for this crime is usually sending the little devil to his room so he can happily play with all his toys located there. I proceed no further with this train of thought.

Then there's the middle-aged couple locked in a heated dispute, their gestures and words painting a vivid picture of their disagreement. Perhaps she didn't need to buy that new outfit. Maybe he wanted to go to the ball game instead of going to the theatre. Oh, the scenarios I concocted for them!

Finally, three teenaged girls walk by giggling and talking, probably planning what they are going to do on the weekend. I am immediately transported back to my own teenage years, and I find myself smiling.

And the fantasies continue as the people walk by.

But the most delightful part of this pastime lies in observing men and women in their natural habitats, socializing in their own unique circles. Let's start with the men.

A group of elderly, retired gentlemen convene at the corner coffee shop around 9:00 a.m. for their weekly get-together. They are dressed in their work clothes, ready for a day of puttering around. Generally a grumpy lot, their faces rarely graced with smiles, they complain about how things aren't like they used to be and how everything is going to hell in a handbasket. Politics, sports, aches and pains, and whatever bothers them at home are the topics of discussion. When their hour is up, they trod on home, wondering what the little woman is making them for lunch.

Now, let's shift our gaze to the women, socializing in a world entirely their own. What a wonderfully different scene this paints. Just the other day, Chuck and I were having lunch in a local restaurant and a gathering of smartly dressed senior ladies was seated at a nearby table.

"God, they are loud," was the comment issued by an annoyed Chuck.

I couldn't help but smile.

"Yes," I replied, "they are loud, and isn't it wonderful these ladies are letting loose and having so much fun?"

These old girls had my full attention, and although I wasn't a part of their circle, I fully enjoyed watching and overhearing their lively chatter. They ordered wine . . . lots of wine. Every conceivable topic was open to discussion, followed by howls of laughter and more wine.

In that moment, I thought to myself, "Women really know how to live at this stage of life. They have devoted their entire lives to the needs of others, and now they realize it is high time they started living for themselves."

I turned to Chuck and said, "I raise my glass to these spirited senior ladies and to all women who have finally decided to raise a little hell and to have some fun, because they have damn well earned it."

There was no comeback response from Chuck.

CHAPTER 4

CHAOS AND ORDER

*When a balance of chaos and order
exists, life becomes interesting.*
L. Pilon

Wild Sex in the Country

As Chuck's retirement marked the beginning of a new chapter in our lives, one in which we embraced a quiet, slower-paced way of living, I found myself slowly falling in love with this rustic paradise. Mother Nature was at her finest, providing us with an ever-evolving drama of the natural world. Just by sitting at our kitchen table, we had front row seats to all her marvels and mysteries.

One day, Chuck's exuberant voice echoed through the house, breaking the peaceful silence.

"Hey Lynn, come and see the deer in the third field."

Chuck's excitement was contagious. I was standing beside him in a flash.

"It looks too wide to be a deer," I mused.

Binoculars were whipped out, and we peered out into the distance. To our surprise, the mysterious creature was a male turkey, his body feathers puffed up, tail feathers fanned out, and his brightly coloured waddle just a swinging. He was really strutting his stuff. Turkey mating season had arrived in Limehouse. With no others in sight, I couldn't help but assume that this was Tommy Turkey rehearsing his courtship dance, eager to perfect his moves for the real event.

You see, just the year before, I had witnessed this awe-inspiring display of sex in the field, and I knew we were in for some major entertainment. All the ingredients—love, lust, and consequences—were in play. I was so excited to watch this movie develop before my very eyes. I remember thinking that I couldn't wait to share the experience with Tammy and Steven. However, their reactions were less enthusiastic than I had hoped for. Their eyes rolled in unison, and I could practically see them mentally adding "find a home for Mom" to their to-do list. I don't know why they think I'm weird. I thought my story of turkey courtship was worthy of a nature documentary. Let me explain.

I told them, in great detail, about the two male turkeys and their two lady friends going through the mating ritual. It was fascinating. The toms had their feathers spread out like peacocks. They danced and strutted around the hens for at least fifteen minutes.

I couldn't resist a cheeky observation, so I commented to Tammy and Steven, "The human race could take some lessons here on foreplay."

Their disgusted response was swift. They plugged their ears so they could hear no more. But my story wasn't finished. When their ears were clear of all obstructions, I continued.

"Finally, the hens said to the toms, 'Oh for God's sake, just get it over with.'"

There was a piercing scream from Steven as he fled the room. "Why?" I ask you. Kids!

And the story continues. As a result of this sexual encounter, one hen, who we named Henrietta, stayed near the house all summer. We watched as her cute day-old chicks—eight of them—grew up to become full-grown, ugly turkeys. It was better than TV. I gave it a five-star rating.

From Green Thumbs to Grocery Runs

The fragrance of recently plowed fields, absorbing the sun's warmth, permeated the air. Spring had made its entrance, and along with it, an ancient, long-buried instinct began to stir within Chuck. A wild idea had taken root in his mind, one that refused to be ignored—he wanted to create a garden. But this was no ordinary garden; it would be a sprawling vegetable patch that aimed to rival the pioneers' agricultural feats. Lynda's talents would come into play as well, preserving fruit, crafting jam and pickles, and freezing vegetables to see us through the long, harsh winter ahead. And then, according to Chuck, there was the added bonus of us toiling together, side by side, in the blazing heat, harvesting this bounty.

What a dumb idea!

Memories of my childhood spent wrestling with stubborn weeds in the family garden were still too vivid. I couldn't fathom this *Little House on the Prairie* lifestyle, and I declared with strong conviction that if he wanted a garden, it was his baby. I wanted no part of it.

Chuck's dream of cultivating this garden became a reality for a couple of years, until he was finally confronted with some cold, hard facts—more food was going to waste than we could consume, and purchasing a ten-pound bag of carrots in the fall was more economical than investing in a packet of seeds in the spring. With this realization, Chuck's garden project was permanently put to bed. However, the desire to live off the land still pulsed within him, and his attention soon turned to another project that would fulfill his pioneer soul.

Spraying For Divorce

In the world of farming, there exists seasons of abundance and seasons of despair. Our farm was no exception. In our inaugural year on this land, our fruit trees bestowed upon us a bounty that could rival the treasures of any orchard. The apples, a symphony of perfection in size, appearance, and taste, could easily have won prizes at the fall fair. However, the saga of our orchard would soon take an unexpected turn in the years that followed.

The second year, the apples were a shadow of their former glory, and by the third, our crop was a complete write-off. It was a dismal scene, small in size, overrun by scale, and infested with worms. Even the deer, known for their foraging prowess, turned up their noses at our pitiful harvest. At this point, we realized that something had to change if we were going to reclaim our orchard's former glory.

Seeking guidance from those who claimed to be experts, we found their advice as barren as a fruitless tree. Perhaps our last hope lay in a dormant oil spray, one of the few legal choices still available. The idea behind this option was simple: by spraying the entire tree in the early spring before the buds opened, the oil and water mixture would smother overwintering insects, kill the eggs, plus, as an added bonus, prevent scale from occurring.

Because this was an unfamiliar endeavour for us, having never used this spray before, I decided, being a woman, to read the instructions to see what the water-to-oil ratio would be. Chuck, on the other hand, being a man, and having just purchased a brand-new sprayer from Canadian Tire, was just itching to try out his new toy.

I settled down on a rock opposite the first apple tree, took out the instruction pamphlet, and proceeded to read. Chuck, with oil and water in hand, was standing on the other side of the tree looking directly at me, waiting to hear the words of wisdom on what the ratio should be. Two minutes passed, a lifetime for gun-slinging, vigilante Chuck. Things had to get done and now, so Chuck decided he would guess at the amount. He had waited long enough. It is interesting to note that Chuck has always been a firm believer in the concept *more* is better, thus the oil-water mixture was mostly made up of oil. He would get rid of those damn insects come hell or, as in this case, low water.

Knee-deep in thought and concentration, I did not realize an ambush lay in store for me. Without warning, Chuck squeezed the trigger on the sprayer and let it rip. Now, this was early spring with very little growth on the tree. Big open spaces were between the branches, and there I was, perched on my rock. As the oil rained down upon me, I was transformed into a living canvas adorned with inky black spots, resembling a piece of abstract art.

Naturally, I was not amused.

Chuck, always quick with a comeback, offered his dubious consolation.

"Oh well," he said, "At least you don't have to worry about getting worms."

(And we wonder why the divorce rate is so high.)

In the weeks that followed, our orchard underwent a remarkable transformation. Chuck's unconventional, oil-heavy assault had, surprisingly, managed to defeat the bug invaders. As the apple trees blossomed, they did so with a newfound vigor, as if grateful for the drastic measures taken to save them. As the months passed, we watched with bated breath as the apples grew, and the moment of truth arrived. The harvest that year exceeded our wildest expectations. The apples were not only free of scale and worms, but were plump, juicy, and more abundant than ever before.

And so, our story continued, a testament to the resilience of nature, and the determination of those who tilled the land. We had weathered the storm, and in doing so, had discovered the true magic of our farm–a place where the impossible could become possible, and where the sweetest victories were born from the most unexpected battles.

Crap Happens

Chuck and I were both raised on farms, but let's face it, when you have spent over four decades in the city, enjoying all its modern conveniences, you tend to forget the demands of carefree rural living. We paid the price for our forgetfulness, but in doing so, we gained some hard-earned wisdom.

My thoughts drift back to that unforgettable day, a couple of years after purchasing our place, when sudsy water and a little extra material, which I won't describe, appeared on the furnace room floor. It was a stark reminder that septic systems require maintenance every two or three years. Our ignorance had finally caught up with us, resulting in the septic tank backing up. A frantic call was made to Steven, "Get over here quick. We have a stinking mess to clean up!"

Leafing through the Yellow Pages (there was no Google back then), I found a septic guy who said he could come out immediately, if we knew where the opening to the tank was. Well, we had a rough idea, but with Chuck frantically digging up half the lawn trying to locate it, I suggested I phone the couple we had bought the place from for this information. This was done, and Bill, the previous owner, gave us directions to the exact spot. After the top was found, we quickly called the poop truck and the fellow arrived. But here is where things got interesting—septic systems have two parts: one for liquids and one for solids. We had to locate the other opening. Luckily, or maybe not, Septic Sam knew exactly where this would be—right in the middle of the interlocking brick patio we had built in front of the hot tub. Tension and an ungodly smell hung heavily in the air, so I did the only sensible thing, I fled the scene and let the men deal with the situation.

The job was completed, and we were good for another three years. I was just grateful this didn't happen when we had a houseful of company.

So, there we were. The line dividing chaos and order had been realigned. Our feet were no longer stuck in this chaotic madness, balance and calm had been restored. Through it all, we learned that even the messiest challenges can be overcome with a bit of new knowledge and a lot of humour. And thank God we had this philosophy, because the next catastrophe was already appearing on the horizon.

The Annoying Visitors

In the peaceful countryside, where the seasons follow a familiar rhythm, there's an unpleasant annual disruption that accompanies the arrival of springtime tourists. Expecting their impending visit, I prepare as best I can for the usual challenges of meeting, greeting, and managing these bothersome intruders. Urban folk know nothing about these callers. They enjoy the onset of warm May weather as they busily clean up the yard, prepare flower beds, and make barbecue plans. But for the rural population, outside work and pleasures are next to impossible, as this month brings a hostile annoyance: the relentless assault of black flies. These tiny winged tormentors descend upon us like a plague, forming a malevolent halo around our heads and following us wherever we go. You can almost hear them sharpening their knives and forks as they descend upon us for a feast of fresh meat.

I've tried countless remedies, touted as sure-fire solutions, to repel these insufferable insects. Head net contraptions only seem to invite them to sneak beneath the mesh, leaving itchy hive-like bites at the nape of your neck. Citronella canisters, smudge pots, Bounce dryer sheets, Deep Woods spray, and even homemade concoctions—none have proven effective against these tiny demons. The only course of action is to resign oneself to their brief but relentless presence. They live their lives with an audacious indifference to our suffering and, thankfully, vanish as mysteriously as they appear. These miniature devils are definitely a nuisance, but one particular year, things took an unexpected turn, spiralling beyond my control and resulting in disastrous consequences. In retrospect, I can now see a certain degree of humour in the situation, but at the time, it was no laughing matter. There are just some experiences where time must pass before we laugh. This was just such an occasion.

It all began with a leaky hot tub, barely a year old. Because it was still under warranty, I figured I would just contact the company to fix the problem, so I called. No response. I called again. Nothing. I was persistent and finally, after several weeks, a service truck pulled up in our driveway. Three technicians, or so they claimed, stumbled out of the vehicle. As these young guys sauntered around the house looking for the tub, I overheard them discussing their drinking escapades the night before. My confidence in the trio fixing this problem plummeted to a level zero. Furthermore, when I realized they had left all tools and equipment in the truck, I knew things would not go well. I was on high alert. Not only were these guys tool-less, they were also clueless. But they were here, and so were the black flies.

With these little black demons swarming around them like a malevolent cloud, Nit, Wit, and Idiot, the names I christened them with, removed the tub's lid and carelessly tossed it down the hill, its final resting place landing close to the pine trees. My dear Chuck, being the accommodating soul that he is, set up smudge pots in an attempt to drive away the relentless flying terrorists. Since the incompetent trio did not have the parts necessary to fix the leak, they decided two of them would leave to get the required supplies. This left one behind guarding the hot tub.

As they were leaving, one of the morons knocked over a smudge pot, sending it rolling downhill, until it collided with the discarded lid, setting it ablaze. Now, I am not sure if they were unaware of this catastrophe taking place or if they just didn't care, but they did not stop to evaluate the situation. They just went on their merry way. Chuck happened to see the fire and ran over, trying to stamp the flames out with his feet. Nit was frozen like a statue, staring in disbelief at what was unravelling before his eyes.

"Get the damn garden hose," yelled Chuck, "before the tree catches fire and spreads to the house."

Still no movement or help from Nit. By sheer luck and quick thinking, Chuck was able to control and put out the fire. When we inquired about replacing the damaged tub cover, the company had the audacity to quote us a staggering $500 for a new one. Suffice it to say, that was one bill we had no intention of paying.

Upon reflection, I'm beginning to think maybe we should show some respect for the black fly population. Despite being unwelcome nuisances, these tiny creatures exhibit a level of predictability and efficiency that contrasts sharply with the erratic behaviour of certain individuals within the human species. Black flies provide a straightforward and tangible model to mimic. They adhere to a reliable schedule. They appear promptly, fulfill their mysterious duties, and depart without overstaying their welcome. There's a certain clarity in their actions—we know where we stand with them.

The events that occurred that day tested not just our patience, but our very mettle. Could we truly survive the rigours of rural life, or would it prove too much for us?

In a moment of despair, I thought, "I can take no more," but I was wrong.

Our ordeal, it seemed, was not yet over.

Where Do You Find a Hero?

The allure of our country retreat had been the promise of relaxation and a little less stress in our lives. However, achieving this dream entailed months of never-ending work, where Chuck and I seemingly defied the laws of time, mastering the art of squeezing thirty hours of work into a mere twenty-four-hour day. But the relentless pursuit of our dream came at a cost—a barrage of renovation-induced headaches and unexpected disasters.

No sooner were old problems fixed or changed than new issues would surface. The pool liner springing a leak, the septic system backing up, and the hot tub lid catching on fire were just a few of the crises we were dealing with. Our sanity was hanging by a thread. We needed a break; a respite from the endless turmoil. That escape came in the form of a weekend booked at the Westin Harbour Castle Hotel in Toronto. This stress-free time off was just what the doctor ordered. How were we to know that our brief getaway would turn into a life-threatening ordeal high above the city.

Upon arriving, the hotel surprised us with an upgrade to a deluxe guest suite on the thirtieth floor, complete with a balcony overlooking Lake Ontario. Could things get any better? It was as if serendipity had graced us with a glimpse of the good life, an opportunity to live like the rich and famous for a precious two days. The prospect of indulging in this unexpected luxury filled me with excitement.

With our hearts full of anticipation, we entered the room, our sanctuary for the weekend. I tossed my purse onto the bed and, without a second thought, slid the security bar upwards from the sliding door to the side of the door frame. I couldn't wait to step out on the balcony and soak in the breathtaking view of the lake, its surface dotted with tiny sailboats. We were on the thirtieth floor, so everything below resembled miniatures. (It is also important to my story to inform you that our balcony wasn't very big, just large enough to accommodate two lawn chairs and a tiny drink table sitting between them.)

Chuck joined me on the balcony, closing the door behind him. Click! Disaster!

I had not snapped the security bar into its bracket on the door frame. Without realizing it, I had more or less left it sitting in midair. When Chuck slammed the door shut, that jolt made the Charlie bar fall back down into its lock position. We could not get back into the room. Panic washed over me as terrifying thoughts raced through my mind. We were too high for anyone to hear us from the balcony, and our *upgraded* room was the only one on this floor with a balcony. There was a strong possibility that we would be out there for some time. No one would be coming to our suite until the next day when housekeeping was scheduled for cleaning. I could even see the newspaper headlines, "Two adults found dead after being locked out on hotel balcony for a week."

I felt sick. To make things even more horrifying, my two big phobias kicked in—a fear of heights and a fear of confined spaces. Bingo. I had a full card.

It was a perfect storm of terror, and I was caught in its grip.

"What will we do?" I gasped.

"Calm down and let me assess the situation," Chuck cautioned, his voice steady and assured.

With nearly fifty years of experience in the window and door industry, he wasn't worried. He knew he could find a solution to this predicament. He searched his pockets and found only two coins, a toonie and a loonie, not exactly tools for breaking and entering. However, a glimmer of hope emerged when he noticed that the bar hadn't fallen squarely into the bracket. It was caught on the edge of the locking mechanism. Chuck bent down and wedged the toonie under the door. By setting the loonie on top of the other coin, he was able to create just enough space to jiggle the door back and forth. For thirty agonizing minutes, he worked to inch the bar away from the bracket until it finally fell free. MacGyver Chuck had saved the day! The door was open! I immediately rushed to the bathroom and threw up, the fear and relief overwhelming me.

In our world full of celebrated heroes, we often overlook the everyday heroes who quietly come to our rescue. Chuck was my hero that day, and I told him so. While it wasn't the perfect start to our getaway, it could have been far worse. Gratitude filled my heart since we still had two days left to recuperate, steady our nerves, and attempt to enjoy the remainder of our time in this luxurious haven. We had to recharge our batteries as, only God knew what lay in wait for us at home on Monday.

I learned important lessons that weekend. Firstly, I never step onto a balcony without leaving the door wide open, and I always carry my purse with a fully charged cell phone whenever I venture out onto a deck. And secondly, but more importantly, I realized heroes can appear at any time and anywhere. When you are lucky enough to have one, you thank God that he or she was there for you when you needed them most.

The Missing Hard Hat

In the world of farming, tales of horrific accidents involving machinery, animals, or sheer foolishness are well known. These stories often end with victims bearing serious injuries or even worse fates. A little common sense could prevent many of these mishaps from occurring. Before Chuck's retirement, his workplace was a bastion of safety. Health and Safety Committee meetings were held religiously, written policies were treated as gospel, and everyone followed the guidelines to the letter, including Chuck. But as soon as retirement beckoned, safety seemed to fade into the rearview mirror of his life, a mysterious transformation neither Chuck nor anyone else could explain.

Chuck's accidents and near misses predominantly revolved around trees and his passion for chainsaws. The allure of cutting fallen timber for firewood holds a special place in his heart, but this Paul Bunyan career can be dangerous. A wise person wears the appropriate personal protective equipment (PPE), but then, not everyone is wise. There are times when Chuck falls into the latter category.

I have had my fair share of encounters with Chuck's lumberjack escapades. There was that memorable day when he tested the sharpness of his chainsaw blade on his own leg. Thankfully, layers of denim first intercepted the blade's hungry bite, and with his finger off the trigger, the speed of the chain had fortunately slowed down somewhat. Though arteries and veins were mercifully spared, a nasty gash remained. A trip to the doctor for stitches was not even a consideration in Chuck's eyes. The cure for the day would be to have the wife tape up the wound as best as she could and just hope that no infection found its way to the site. The following day, he grudgingly limped to the Farmers' Co-op and bought chaps to wear when using this weapon. A case of *better late than never*, perhaps?

But Chuck's tree safety education was far from over. His legs were now covered with PPE, but what about the other parts of his body? Did he have everything covered? Of course not. Might as well wait until after the fact before we make safety a priority. I knew it was only a matter of time before I would play doctor again, taping up some area of his body, and I was not wrong.

One morning, after riding around the perimeter of our property on his ATV, Chuck informed me of another job that required his immediate attention. He had spotted a forty-foot dead elm that had been pulled out of the earth by its roots. Rather than falling directly to the ground, it was entangled high above in the branches of another nearby tree. It was a peculiar sight, one that whispered a potential hazard if left unattended.

"Better get that tree down before it falls on its own and hits someone on the head," he declared with an air of caution.

Oh, the irony of that statement.

However, to Chuck's credit, he had meticulously thought the project out before proceeding with this daring venture. With one end of the chain securely anchored to the drawbar on the tractor and the other end attached firmly around the base of the captive tree's roots, his strategy was put into action. Now, in a perfect world, the tree would have smoothly pulled along the ground behind the tractor until it was far enough away from the supporting tree, where at that point it would have gently fallen to the ground. But this is not a perfect world. Chuck started the tractor, the chain tightened, and the tree did a complete somersault, with the top branches hitting him squarely on the top of his head.

I was on the veranda, and I saw this old man with a rather glazed look in his eyes staggering up the driveway. Blood was pouring down the side of his face. Of course, it was Chuck. Did he go to the doctor for stitches? Was the possibility of a concussion ruled out? Don't be silly. I washed away the blood, bandaged it as best I could, and he was good to go.

"Now, where was his hard hat?" one might ask.

That brand-new puppy has been sitting on a shelf in the garage for the past fifteen years, collecting dust. There is not a scratch or a dent on it. I wonder why?

Idiot or Genius: That Is the Question

But perhaps Chuck's most ingenious caper, one that he not only survived, but also emerged unscathed from, was the foolhardy scheme he hatched up for harvesting apples and pears. Our fruit trees, nestled on the side of a hill, presented a challenging terrain for reaching the bountiful crop with a simple ladder. When we first arrived at the farm, it was still feasible to scale the trees or position a ladder partially up their trunks, but as time passed, the trees grew taller, and Chuck and I grew older. The agility we had once possessed for climbing had waned. During this particular year, our trees bore an abundance of tantalizing fruit. I proposed limiting our harvest to the lower branches and leaving the rest for the deer, who could undoubtedly smell the feast from miles away. There was no conceivable way we could consume all those apples, and even if we gave most of them away, I had no desire to risk life and limb picking every last one. Yet, Chuck remained undeterred.

His pioneer spirit said, "Harvest all those pears and apples, and we shall stock our pantry with pies, jams, applesauce, preserves, and God knows what else for the winter."

Furthermore, he rhymed off a list of people we could share our bounty with. There was no stopping him.

Now, Chuck possesses a collection of Tonka toys and a vivid imagination—assets that can be truly wonderful, albeit occasionally unpredictable. On this occasion, Chuck went to the drawing board of his mind. You see, everything on our farm bears a name, even Chuck's equipment. There's Little Blue, his trusty tractor; RW, the reliable red wagon; and Case, yet another dependable tractor. With determination in his eyes, Chuck set his ingenious plan into motion. He expertly hitched the wagon to Little Blue and manoeuvred it up the hill until RW stood right alongside the target tree. After dismounting from Little Blue, he strategically positioned a substantial chunk of wood behind one of its rear tires to serve as an additional braking device. (How safety conscious can one get?) Then, with precision, he climbed aboard Case and carefully guided it toward the back of RW. When everything was aligned just right, he raised the front-end bucket on Case, gracefully hoisting the rear end of RW until the wagon rested perfectly level. This feat left the back two wheels of RW dangling a few feet in midair. His homemade scaffold, in all its glory, was in place. I couldn't help but admit that this unconventional apple-picking platform looked remarkably strong and secure. Maybe it would work.

Chuck was determined to harvest the fruit at the very top of the tree. To achieve this, he placed a sturdy six-foot ladder inside the wagon and began to climb it. I must confess that I was on the verge of a heart attack. Did this man possess a death wish? As he ascended higher, the ladder swayed more and more, and before I knew it, there were two senior citizens inside the wagon—one precariously balanced on the ladder, while the other clung to it in a desperate attempt to maintain stability. It took me just a couple of minutes to realize that this was a harebrained idea. I won't go into detail describing the heated discussion that followed between the two of us. Suffice it to say, I retreated from the scene, leaving Chuck to continue his daring fruit-picking operation. I just couldn't be a part of this suicide mission. I did, however, take the precaution of opening the windows, just in case I needed to hear his cries for help. Thankfully, everything proceeded without a hitch.

As it stands, the jury is still out on whether this escapade qualifies Chuck as an eccentric genius or a fearless fool. Men are in his corner, thinking he is a genius, while women tend to favour the fool opinion. Regardless of the verdict, I am eternally grateful for all the overtime Chuck's guardian angels have invested in overseeing his actions. They have kept him alive and well. And so, we carry on, living by the motto, "Let the adventure continue."

CHAPTER 5

OTHER FAMILY MEMBERS

Four paws on the floor bring happiness to your door.
L. Pilon

"Mom, Can We Have a Dog?"

I grew up on a farm where the prevailing wisdom dictated that cats were meant for the barn and dogs belonged outdoors. Each had its job: cats kept the mouse population in check and dogs herded cattle. Our household had a steadfast rule: "No animals allowed in the house."

I carried this unwavering belief into the early years of our marriage, but my children, and a husband with a profound love for all creatures, had a different vision in mind.

"Can we have a dog, please, Mom, pleeeeease? We promise to walk, feed, and look after him," was their heartfelt plea.

Now, I'm not a mean mother, but I knew deep down in my heart that the novelty of taking care of this animal would soon wear off. I was not willing to shoulder the full responsibility and care for this lovable four-legged pet, and so, I said, "No."

But this firm denial would only serve to postpone the inevitable.

One summer day, Charlie nonchalantly wandered into our yard.

"Maria's cat is here, Mom," Tammy excitedly yelled, letting me, plus the entire street, know this great news.

Every night we would hear our neighbour, Maria, call her cat, "Come Charlie, kitty, kitty," so we knew his name.

This cat demonstrated exceptional intelligence. He became a daily fixture in our yard, approaching our kids with an innate understanding of how to melt hearts—purring and rubbing himself against their legs—fully aware of his endearing tactics. It seemed that leaving our safe, happy environment was the last thing on his mind. After persistent appeals from Chuck, Tammy, and Steven, I reluctantly surrendered on one condition: if Maria would part with Charlie, we would offer him a home.

Two excited kids and one nervous, uncertain me, who wasn't sure we should even dare ask Maria to give up her pet, approached her door.

Marie answered with a smile and a perplexed look on her face as she took in the picture of the three of us plus one contented sleeping cat snuggling in Tammy's arms.

"Maria, can we have Charlie?" Tammy blurted out.

The suspense was killing the kids.

Maria had a blank look.

"He has been at our place for weeks," Steven quickly added.

Still no comment from a very confused Maria.

I thought to myself, "This isn't going well."

"We'll take good care of him," Tammy pleaded as she held Charlie up for her to see.

Then a big laugh erupted from Maria.

"Yes, I have a cat named Charlie," she said, "but he is a marmalade-coloured cat. This handsome tabby you are holding isn't mine. I've seen this cat hanging around the street for some time. I don't think he has a home."

That was all the kids needed to hear. A cheer went out, and I knew that I was dead in the water.

This unexpected adoption, which would forever alter our lives, went surprisingly smoothly. We opened the door, and Charlie confidently strolled right in, claiming his place in our hearts and our home.

After Charlie, our home was never pet-free. I did, however, win one small battle—we never got a dog. Over the past four decades, stray felines have continued to seek refuge at the Pilon home, and they have always been welcomed with open arms. We have had not just one cat, not just two cats, not just three cats, but often four cats in our home at the same time. Presently, we have four, all strays who have found us.

I must confess, though, that Chuck and I have made a decision: at our age, no more *new* cats will be adopted. Good Lord, the felines might outlive us. This news bulletin has brought about a great sense of relief from our kids, as they have visualized inheriting a bunch of new dependants. (Steven already has three cats and Tammy's kids are allergic to them.) So, with that declaration in mind, I will recount the story of one of our most recent and probably our last addition.

From Stray to Stay

Last summer, a scrawny, half-starved kitten, perhaps only four or five months old, came into our sights while prowling on our property. Living in the vast expanse of the countryside, where animals have ample room to roam, it was only a matter of time before curiosity drew this little black-and-white feline closer to our house.

In those early days, she was a wild, untamed spirit with no social graces, leading us to believe she might be one of our neighbour's barn cats. She regarded humans with suspicion, constantly on high alert for any signs of danger. During the initial weeks, she would dart away the moment we appeared on the scene. In an effort to at least put a little meat on her bones, we started leaving food out on our front porch. As the weeks passed and fall approached, Kitty (that's what we called her) began to trust us, and although she was always keenly aware of her surroundings, she would tolerate us watching her eat. Eventually, she permitted us to pet her, and before we knew it, she was demanding to have her belly rubbed and her ears scratched. She had come a long way.

Turning Kitty into an indoor cat was out of the question, primarily due to the aggressive reactions of our two-year-old cat Missy, who had hissy fits whenever she caught sight of Kitty through the window. On the other hand, our fourteen-year-old grandpa cat Ben just didn't have the energy to get worked up over this possible intruder. Nevertheless, the verdict was in. Kitty would have to make her home outside.

As time passed, our concern grew about how Kitty would weather the colder months. To address this dilemma, we decided to search on Amazon to see what type of shelter was available for our little girl. Given the recent skyrocketing surge in real estate prices, it came as no surprise to us that pet houses were far from budget-friendly. Furthermore, there was a glaring absence of suitable cat houses on the market. This led us to consider an upgrade: a doghouse.

After some research, we stumbled upon a Giantex plastic doghouse measuring 34" x 30" x 32" that had been designed for a fifty-pound dog. Chuck, with his unwavering belief in top-quality purchases, didn't hesitate or haggle over the asking price. The house was immediately ordered, with Amazon Prime promising a two-day delivery date. I couldn't help but comment to Chuck that this doghouse was the perfect castle for our petite five-pound cat, and that it was even big enough to accommodate her extended feline family, if she so desired. Chuck, however, remained silent on that notion.

Clearly, this doghouse came equipped with many built-in comforts, boasting an elevated floor to keep water at bay, a well-ventilated design to regulate temperatures, deluxe construction, and a list of never-ending features. The doghouse arrived as per schedule in a nice flat 36" x 32" x 8" high box. Assembly was required. According to the accompanying manual, the building of this little home could be completed by one person in only thirty minutes.

Being very wise and having learned from past experiences, I immediately vanished from sight, leaving Chuck to tackle this advertised *easy* task of constructing Miss Kitty's new residence. Call me psychic, but I couldn't help but anticipate the impending chaos. An hour later, my foreboding proved correct when an exasperated and irritable Chuck emerged from the scene of the battle.

"What kind of idiot writes these instructions?" he snapped; his frustration palpable.

Now, I must come to Chuck's defence here; those instructions were undoubtedly the work of inept authors. After an entire hour of teamwork, two people finally managed to complete the project. However, in Chuck's discerning view, the house needed a series of adjustments and thoughtful additions to make it truly habitable for his little feline friend. His concern for Kitty's safety led him to make the entrance smaller, creating a cozy and secure space. Chuck even decided to attach a wooden shelf, or as he humorously referred to it—a loft—to one inside wall in case Kitty desired a higher vantage point to survey her kingdom. To enhance Kitty's comfort, a plush carpet was installed, transforming the dwelling into a palace fit for the most celebrated of cats.

Where would we place this fine establishment? Location, location, location is everything in the real estate market. We needed to get the perfect spot—a sheltered, pristine area close to our house. The desired lot was located and move-in day arrived.

Chuck was so excited. He couldn't wait for Kitty to curl up in this abode he had so lovingly assembled. But Kitty was playing hard to please. She walked over to it, did not enter, gave it one sniff, turned, and with tail held high, she left the building.

A very disappointed Chuck stood in disbelief. He had worked so hard on this project. He would not give up.

"Hey Lynn," he called, "get some treats and put them in the house. Maybe that will entice Kitty to go inside."

A trail of cat nibblies was spread from the entrance to the very back of the house. Hours passed, and finally Kitty, either out of curiosity or perhaps because she could smell the food, ambled back towards the house.

Chuck was beside himself with anticipation.

But this little kitten was street, or should I say, *barn* smart. She would not put herself in a cornered, unsafe position. Lying on the ground just beyond the threshold of the house, she extended her paw, reaching for the tantalizing treats within her grasp. To our dismay, Kitty's move in-date came and went, with no cat inside the fancy house's walls.

As the days rolled on, we continued to wonder about Kitty's nocturnal adventures. Although we didn't know where she disappeared to at night, her predictable return each morning for food and affection made it clear that she had assumed control of our household. She was definitely calling the shots. One morning, however, she failed to make her customary appearance. We were really worried. It was then we realized, whether we were ready to admit it or not, that Kitty had become an integral part of our family. But the following evening, an unexpected twist of events occurred. Chuck opened our garage doors, and out strolled a nonchalant Kitty. She had been accidentally locked inside for two days.

Apparently, the garage was to her liking, as she immediately claimed it as her own and moved right in. I just shook my head. At least there was no assembly, no renovating nor decorating required with this abode. Well, that statement was not entirely true. Chuck had to make Miss Kitty comfortable. Sleeping arrangements varied from a box full of straw to a cozy place on the tractor seat. Food, water, and a litter box were all at her disposal, ensuring her every need was met. To top it off, a heater was supplied for her comfort during the colder nights. Depending on the weather and her mood, the door was opened daily, granting her the freedom to explore as she pleased. She was usually back within an hour. I smiled when I watched her faithfully follow Chuck like a loyal little dog, accompanying him on trips to the mailbox or going to the machine house. This little feline was bringing so much joy into our lives.

For a time, it seemed like Kitty had the perfect life, with her physical needs attended to and a vet visit in the near future to fulfill her medical requirements. Her emotional and social needs were lovingly met by two doting seniors, and she retained her cherished freedom to come and go as she pleased. It was, by all accounts, a blissful existence.

But things were about to change for Kitty.

Consequences

Kitty continued her daily outside jaunts according to her schedule, but she always returned to the comforts of her heated home, where fresh water and an abundance of food were available at all times. She had us well-trained.

But one fateful day in early January, the unexpected happened. Kitty didn't return after her usual afternoon walk, sending us into a panic as we envisioned the dangers that lurked in the countryside. Coyotes and prowling tomcats haunted our thoughts, and a thousand worries raced through our minds. But, five days later, much to our relief, the cat came back. We thought she was a goner, but the cat came back! It seemed like she had beaten the odds, but if we had been a little more observant, we might have detected the smug look on her face.

As we moved into February, Kitty's appetite reached insatiable levels, leaving us baffled.

"I swear, that cat is eating enough for six," commented Chuck.

We were indeed very suspicious of our little girl. Had she had an affair on her five-day getaway? Although she hadn't packed any bags when she left, we strongly believed she had brought back some baggage.

As time went on, it became apparent we needed to make some adjustments. The unused cat/dog house we had purchased in the fall was relocated to the garage, in hopes Kitty would choose it as her nursery. We moved it in early to give her time to adjust to its presence, and we prepared it with care, laying a soft bed of straw inside. The rest was left to Kitty. Approximately two weeks before her expected date, we curtailed Kitty's outdoor excursions to avoid the possibility of finding frozen kittens in an outdoor hideaway she might choose. Then, the big day arrived, and she gave birth in the doghouse, just as we had anticipated—four of them—two grey kittens, one black kitten, and one black and white with a bit of marmalade colouring thrown in for good measure.

I anxiously observed the birthing process, but to my surprise, Kitty seemed uncertain about what to do with her newborns. Worried about the frigid temperatures, we brought Kitty and her new family, along with her litter box, food, water, and a box filled with straw into the living room. We gently rubbed the little guys to get some life back into them, and then placed the box of kittens in front of the fireplace. We hoped for the best. But Kitty's maternal instincts had not yet kicked in, causing her to inadvertently roll over on her babies, prompting them to cry out. For the next few hours, our routine involved rescuing the kittens from beneath their mother and placing them back on her belly. Eventually, Kitty realized these youngsters were her responsibility, so she better take on the role of being a mother.

Loving homes were found for all the kittens, and after an interesting and extended adjustment period for all feline residents, Kitty has become a cherished, permanent indoor addition to our home. There was only one task left to complete. There would be no future babies for Kitty. A trip to the vet's was on the agenda for her.

Max, the Cat

Pets, those four-legged, furry companions, have a remarkable way of weaving their way into our hearts and homes. They quickly cease to be just animals, and before we know it, they have become cherished members of our families. Although they all engage in behaviour that we find ingenious and amazing, what really sets them apart from each other are their distinct personalities, individual quirks, and unique traits. As I look back over our pet years, there is one feline who stole my heart a little more than the others. Meet Max.

Back in 2007, a stray cat gave birth to a litter of kittens at our workplace. The mother cat and her kittens were captured and lovingly cared for until the time came to find forever homes for all of them, including mama. Max, a cute little black-and-white charmer, found his way into our lives. He was the sole cat in our house for five months until one fateful day when another stray kitten wandered in through the bay doors. This little, totally black feline boldly walked right into my office and demanded to be petted. Well, what else could I do? So, just like that, Max had a playmate. According to the vet, they were both around the same age, and they bonded immediately despite their vastly different temperaments.

Ben was gentle, relaxed, and laid back, and I truly believe he was unionized as he did nothing around the house to help Max. Max, on the other hand, was the complete opposite. He was the worker, the worrier, the mom, taking on all the responsibilities of ensuring everyone was safe and accounted for. He became the unofficial security cat, guarding the house when we were away, eagerly welcoming us at the door upon our return, and overseeing any visitors or workers in our home. His vigilant watch would often unnerve tradesmen, and one day, a plumber, bewildered by Max's scrutiny, could take it no longer.

"Would you put that cat in another room?" he begged. "He's starting to give me the creeps."

Not all supervisors are appreciated.

But perhaps Max's most extraordinary feat was related to my health. Apparently, during my sleep, I would stop breathing several times a night, and according to Chuck, in his own intuitive way, Max would gently touch my cheek with his paw until I stirred and resumed breathing. This went on for several months, and it was only after Chuck revealed this to me that I realized how Max had been a silent guardian of my health.

My comment to Chuck upon hearing this information was, "Well, thank God for Max. One of these days, I might wake up dead."

"Oh, don't worry," my not-overly-concerned husband replied, "if Max isn't there, I'll just give you a little poke."

Shortly after that conversation, I decided to invest in a CPAP machine to address my sleep apnea. After all, Max needed less stress.

But there was one occasion when I felt perhaps my boys were not living up to the standard of being great cats. On this particular evening, as I sat watching TV, a subtle movement by the corner of my chair caught my eye. To my surprise and dismay, a tiny deer mouse was staring right back at me. I immediately reacted to this uninvited guest with a mix of astonishment and fear, for I've never been particularly fond of mice. In fact, to put it in stronger language, "I hate mice."

With me now standing on my chair, and my three male companions—two feline furballs and my human, Chuck—sprawled out on the couch, blissfully napping, I knew I had to act fast.

"There is a mouse in the house!" I screeched.

However, my cry for help only elicited a mild reaction from Chuck, who failed to understand what I was so upset about. After all, it was just a little mouse. The cats must have shared his view on this vermin situation, as they did not stir. In hindsight, I realize that if I'd said, "Treat time," I might have seen a different level of enthusiasm from them.

To calm me down and to shut me up, Chuck decided to take matters into his own hands. Armed with a paper towel, his choice of weapon, he attempted to apprehend the elusive trespasser. But because the mouse was either too nimble or Chuck was too slow, no capture took place. I glanced over at Ben and Max, who remained sprawled out, peacefully asleep, seemingly unaffected by the commotion.

In a somewhat sarcastic tone, I remarked, "Those cats are top-notch mousers."

Chuck, in an attempt to protect his boys' reputations, decided to give them a chance to prove their mousing skills. He gently lifted both cats off their perches and placed them on the floor, ensuring they had a prime view of the safari taking place in our rec room. However, even with the cats now staring at this terrified little creature, there was still no action on their part.

The turning point came when the mouse almost ran over Max's feet, setting off a flurry of activity. The mouse darted under the treadmill machine, and the two cats began circling, or as Chuck put it, *walking the perimeter*. It was a suspenseful showdown. Eventually, the mouse made a break for it, but unfortunately, this was not a smart move on his part. He was now face to face with the mighty lions. In a dramatic effort, this trembling little mouse stood on its hind legs, bravely confronting its formidable foes. I couldn't believe what I was seeing as I witnessed this David and Goliath scene transpire right before my eyes. In the end, Chuck managed to grab the mouse by its tail, swiftly opened the patio door, and tossed the little intruder outside.

"If that little guy is that brave or that stupid, he deserves to live," was Chuck's comment.

Whether the mouse succumbed to fright or lived to share his tale with others, one thing was certain—we had no more mouse encounters that fall in our house.

Chuck summed up the whole experience by announcing, "My boys are lovers not fighters, and that's not a bad thing." The verdict was in.

Over the years, pets have enriched our lives in countless ways, teaching us about unconditional love, loyalty, and the simple joys of life. They remind us that the world is a better place with them by our side, and we, in turn, have the privilege of creating a home that is warmer, happier, and infinitely more colourful because of their presence.

Molly's House

In the quiet corners of our lives, where the line between the wild and the domestic blurs into harmony, a captivating story transpired. This tale begins with Chuck, a man whose boundless affection for all animals led him to embrace an unexpected companion: a pigeon. Now, I've never been particularly fond of birds, especially pigeons, but fate had its own designs for us that summer. Who would suspect this avian acquaintance would become the central character in a heartwarming narrative that would redefine our notions of love, dedication, and the extraordinary lengths we would go for an unexpected feathered friend.

The summer of 2015 set the stage for our story. Chuck discovered a pigeon in our backyard nursing a broken leg, grounded and vulnerable. Immediately, Chuck's protective instincts kicked into high gear. What if other creatures—a prowling cat or a cunning fox—came across this fragile bird, deeming it a tasty snack? The bird was a sitting duck, or should I say, a sitting pigeon. Chuck helped it crawl to the wood pile so it would be relatively safe from predators, but it still needed care in order to survive. Chuck gave it bird food left over from the winter feeders and water every day, and he talked to the pigeon. (He soon became quite fluent in *pigeon*). We called her Molly.

Molly's antics and her well-being soon became topics of conversation for us. Every day over coffee, I would ask Chuck what Molly knew that morning, and apparently, they had quite long chats, as Chuck always had lots to tell me. After a month or so, Molly was able to fly again. She would eat and then fly away for a few hours, but she always returned at night. Molly had two bands on her legs, so she obviously belonged to someone, but Chuck, not wanting to know this information, made a point of not checking that out. His view was, if she was a homing pigeon, her GPS was totally off.

Summer turned into fall, and when the cold weather arrived, Molly flew into the machine house where Chuck keeps his tractors and farm equipment. It appeared she wanted to take permanent residency there. We left the doors open so she could leave, but Molly had no desire to go back into the great beyond. She seemed quite content with her new surroundings, and she was staying put. I was not overly happy about this turn of events, as pigeons crap a lot, but Chuck stood firmly in Molly's corner, so Molly stayed. I threw tarps over the tractors and equipment to try to minimize the damage I knew would surely result from having this tenant.

As time went by, due to lack of exercise plus food constantly at hand, Molly started looking like a turkey.

I said to Chuck, "That pigeon is getting fat. She hasn't got a neck anymore."

Naturally, Chuck spoke up in Molly's defence.

"She is just fluffing up her feathers."

But I must have hit a nerve, as Chuck decided that perhaps he wasn't feeding her the proper food. When in doubt, Google for answers. Did you know that the internet has a ton of information on pigeons? The correct diet was found, *premium* pigeon food was ordered, and a delivery was made to our front door two days later.

After a very cozy, worry-free winter, Molly began to get restless. Spring was in the air, and she began to get curious about the world beyond the machine house. She started to venture outside, first taking ten-minute flights once a day and then increasing both the length of time and the frequency. Chuck would leave the door open in the morning, and Molly would come and go as she pleased. Each afternoon, she would fly back into the building, the door was closed, and all would continue as before.

It was at this time I suggested to Chuck that Molly should have her own house, as I had just cleaned poop off the floors, shelves, and everything else that wasn't covered by tarps in a two-story, thirty-four-foot by sixty-foot building, and I wasn't doing it again. It was truly amazing how well that bird's constitution worked. Chuck had a mission.

He immediately started to work on the blueprints for Molly's house. Now, Molly was downsizing drastically, which was a concern for Chuck, but he would make up for that in other ways. Her house would have style. He located two long narrow windows that would let in lots of natural light and one small slider window that would be perfect for her arrivals and departures. All he needed to do was build a landing strip on either side of the window. Walls were erected, a roof put on and shingled, windows and a door installed. A new product at Home Depot was spotted—floor panels with Styrofoam attached to plywood. It would keep Molly's wee feet warm in the winter. What a great idea! Material was bought and installed. The building was painted. All that was left to do was to insulate and plywood the inside walls. Things were moving right along.

As the construction of Molly's house neared completion, an unexpected turn of events added a bittersweet note to Chuck and Molly's remarkable journey. One fateful day, Molly returned with a suitor, a charming grey and white pigeon who had captured her heart. Chuck wasted no time shooing away this amorous interloper. There was no darn way he was allowing any of that type of nonsense in his building. But love, as they say, knows no boundaries, and the very next day, Molly took flight, following her heart into the world she was destined for.

As Chuck put it, "A bird has to do what a bird has to do."

With Molly's departure, this extraordinary chapter in our lives drew to a close, leaving behind a treasury of cherished memories that have left an indelible mark on our hearts. Molly, the pigeon who defied all odds, enriched our lives with her presence. Chuck's unwavering care and devotion ensured that Molly not only survived but thrived, transforming our backyard into a sanctuary of love and compassion. Their heartwarming journey reminds us that sometimes, the most extraordinary friendships are the ones we least expect.

And what became of Molly's house? Well, that summer, it echoed with the laughter of grandkids using it as a playhouse and then from that winter onward it has been used to store snow tires and lawn furniture. But no matter what purpose or use this building serves, it will always be known as Molly's House.

Nothing Is Free

A few of our friends have jokingly suggested that our methods of acquiring and caring for our pets might be a tad outlandish. I'll readily admit, our animals—be they wild or domesticated—enjoy a rather luxurious life on our farm. Nevertheless, I firmly maintain that we're no more unconventional than the average animal enthusiast. Across all ages, people spare no effort in ensuring the happiness of their furry companions, and for good reason—it brings joy to both parties involved. Parents, in particular, will move mountains to fulfill their children's dreams of pet ownership. My brother Dennis and his wife, Donna, immediately pop up in my mind as a perfect example of this. I remember their journey into the realm of pet ownership. The desire for a furry little friend ran deep in their household, so a cute little kitten was brought home from the local pet shop. Bev and Stacey, their two young daughters, were so excited. What would they call this precious little creature? After much debate, they settled on the name, He/She.

"Why such a strange name?" one might wonder.

Well, the answer is both simple and logical. You see, Dennis, raised on a farm like me, couldn't quite determine the feline's gender, so he covered all possibilities. (I can't believe we are related.)

Life seemed content with He/She until an unexpectant situation arouse requiring drastic changes. It appeared that Stacey might be allergic to cats. A heart-wrenching realization dawned upon them: perhaps their home might not be the ideal place for He/She to stay. So began a journey of tough decisions and even tougher farewells as they sought a new abode for their cherished companion.

For a couple of years, this family reluctantly lived in a pet-free house, as Dennis had convinced his daughters that their health depended on it. But, as the summer of 1994 arrived and the family embarked on a fateful vacation, destiny would soon take an unexpected turn.

A trip to the East Coast seemed innocent enough and was eagerly anticipated by all. Viewing breathtaking scenery, seeing the colourful buildings, enjoying fresh lobster, walking along the beaches, and collecting interesting seashells were all part of the Connells' itinerary. These wishes and desires were all accomplished. It was an amazing holiday.

When the family returned home, Bev and Stacey washed the beautiful seashells they had gathered, admired them, and put them away where all good souvenirs go—in a box in the basement. However, the girls had not quite forgotten them. A plot was just waiting to be uncovered.

A few weeks later, they said to their dad, "We should put those beautiful shells we collected into a tank and get some fish." Now really, how much work can fish be? You don't have to walk them. You don't have to spend a fortune on vaccinations every year. They don't shed hair all over the place, nor do they scratch or chew the furniture. They are the perfect pet, if you have to have a pet. So that day, Dennis took the family down to the pet shop to pick out some fish and a bowl. Not an expensive undertaking . . . or so he thought. The girls chose a twenty-gallon tank that cost $125.

"Well, let's pick out the fish," said a shaken Dennis.

"Oh, you can't do that," replied the sales clerk. "You will have to take the tank home and set it up first. You will also want some gravel to put on the bottom of the tank."

So, Bev and Stacey excitedly decided on the size, shape, and colour of the gravel as Dennis dug into his pocket for another $25.

But the sales clerk was just warming up.

"Have you a proper stand to set this tank on?" he asked. "You realize that when this tank is full of water, it will weigh at least 200 pounds."

"We have a stand," Dennis quickly assured him.

But unfortunately, this was not so. When Donna and Dennis scrutinized their table at home, they realized it could not possibly support the tank's weight.

Back to the store.

"How much is that stand?" asked an increasingly poorer Dennis.

"Sixty-five dollars," came the reply.

Believing they could get a better price and quality table elsewhere, the foursome left the shop empty-handed. Donna's mission was to phone the other pet shops in town to compare prices. This research showed that the store they had been dealing with had the best deals, so back the family traipsed to pick up the stand, and there was $65 less in Dennis's wallet. The tank was finally put together, filled with water, and the gravel was installed. But something was missing.

Stacey broke the silence by saying, "Dad. It looks awfully bare. We should get some ornaments."

So an embarrassed Dennis returned to the store for the fourth time that day. He was welcomed with open arms. A 'No Fishing' sign, a skull, and a sunken ship were purchased for $25.

"Bring in a sample of the water tomorrow, and I'll check the pH level for you," said the helpful clerk.

The next morning, three excited Connells returned to the store, sample in hand, only to be informed that the pH level was too high. However, not to worry, for six dollars they could buy some drops to bring the pH down to an acceptable reading. So the drops were added, the seashells attractively positioned, the fluorescent light put in place, and the tank was a beautiful sight to behold. The family marvelled at what had been accomplished in only five trips to the pet store at the cost of $246. Remember, there were no fish yet.

The next day, a second sample of water was tested. The pH level was worse than the previous trip.

When the desired results were not attained on the third day, a frustrated salesman said to Donna, "You didn't by any chance put seashells in the tank, did you?"

This was definitely a mistake.

That evening the twenty gallons of water were emptied, the tank washed, the gravel rinsed, the water replaced, and the whole process of testing the fresh water began again.

Trip number eight yielded the same results—the pH level was too high. By now, the sales clerk was starting to feel sorry for this family. Because they were generously contributing to his holiday fund for the coming year, he suggested they borrow his tester, and when the water was right, they could bring it back and buy the fish. But all did not go well. On her second time testing the water, Stacey dropped the tester, and it broke into little pieces. Another trip back to the store, plus $8 to replace the clerk's tester.

An exhausting week of daily testing followed before the water was finally deemed fit for fish. Pet day had arrived! Bev however, being a typical twelve year old, could not accompany her family on this momentous occasion as she was busy socializing with friends, so Donna, Dennis, and Stacey returned to the pet shop to buy their fish. Being fair-minded, the three each picked out two fish: six fish for $20.

The next day, Bev chose her fish, four in number. But wait! That meant she had two more fish than Stacey—not fair. Solution: six fish in total were purchased to even things up. By the way, those cost my brother another twenty bucks. Does the story end there? Oh no, this was just the beginning. Four fish died within the first week from overfeeding, and a fifth one met a messy death when it was sucked up by the filtering system. Ammonia levels in the water skyrocketed due to the food decaying, and bacteria formed. The solution to this problem naturally involved more work and more money. And finally, four more fish, a more exotic type, were acquired to the tune of $40 to replace the dearly departed.

Since Dennis's family is a typical one, it goes without saying that the kids lost interest in this whole fish scene and Donna was stuck with the weekly job of treating the water with chemicals, washing all the ornaments, changing the water monthly, and so on. And Dennis, well he is still trying to figure out how those little fish cost him close to $500 which in *1994* was a tidy little sum.

"So, what happened to all that equipment and fish related accessories?" you might ask. Well, a few years later, a customer at Dennis's garage sale bought the lot for forty bucks.

CHAPTER 6

FAMILY GATHERINGS

We may not be crazy, but sometimes I wonder.
L. Pilon

That Magical Time of Year

Snow on rooftops, shoppers rushing around like caffeinated squirrels, and the air thick with excitement—yes, the Christmas season has arrived. As I sit here, gazing at my neighbour's festive light extravaganza, I can't help but wonder how I went from the wide-eyed child eagerly anticipating Santa's visit to the senior who contemplates serving venison at the Christmas meal, just so I won't have to listen to another rendition of "Rudolph the Red-Nosed Reindeer." Clearly, the magic of the season, for me, has transformed in various ways with each passing decade.

Back in the day, when I was knee-high to a snowman, Christmas was the ultimate joyride. Presents were the golden tickets to happiness, and the mere thought of unwrapping that special gift could keep me awake for nights on end.

In my youthful years, December was a flurry of activity—decking the halls and hanging the balls; baking enough cookies to induce a sugar coma; searching for, locating, and cutting down the perfect tree; crafting and wrapping gifts. Your senses would almost explode as you took in all the sights and smells of the season. Fast-forward to today, and I find myself daydreaming about a quiet Christmas Eve church service rather than meeting with friends or praying that the clock strikes 10:00 p.m. to signify closing time at every festive gathering I attend. The ornaments that once adorned my Christmas tree with meticulous care now seem like relics from a bygone era, and the idea of a white Christmas has lost its charm. I've had my fair share of snow up to my arse; I don't need any more.

How did I, as an excited little girl, transform into someone who contemplates the end of poor old Rudolph? Join me as I peel back the layers of my Christmas pasts, each chapter exposing the wonder and charm of a certain era.

The First Sign of Christmas

As a kid, the magical countdown to Santa's arrival wasn't marked by calendar dates but by the appearance of our Christmas tree. The thrill, the bubbling anticipation—it all hinged on Dad and my sister Betty's success at finding the perfect little evergreen. With horses harnessed to the trusty flatbed sleigh, they ventured into the woods, determined to capture the best tree ever. Every year, without exception, the mission was successfully accomplished, and a flawless specimen, as perceived by four delighted children, took its designated spot in our living room. The years raced by, and this cherished holiday ritual continued without incident, until one fateful December when things didn't go exactly as planned.

The day for the annual tree hunt had finally dawned, and Betty, revelling in the joy of this cherished tradition, beckoned to her fiancé, Dave.

"Dave, come join Dad and me to get our tree. It'll be fun."

But Dave was not so sure. After all, he had absolutely no experience with horses, and those super-sized farm animals were certainly a tad intimidating. However, torn between not wanting to disappoint Betty and the desire to make a stellar impression on his future father-in-law, he reluctantly agreed to go along for the ride.

Everything went well until they arrived at their destination. Dad hopped off the sleigh and handed the reins to Dave, who was now, whether he liked it or not, in charge of two very fine specimens of horse flesh. A nervous Dave stood there, and all was calm until Dad CRANKED up the chainsaw to cut down the chosen tree. The horses bolted and Dave's face turned as white as the newly fallen snow. But there was really no chance of any disaster happening, as this was December in Grey County—the snow was up to the horses' bellies. I'm not sure whether it was Dad's laughter or the jolt he felt as the horses lunged forward that haunts Dave more, but he never again went on this trip.

As a parent, pursuing the perfect Christmas tree remained an exciting family tradition, but the method of accomplishing this festive task had undergone a significant transformation. The idyllic image of a horse-drawn sleigh was replaced by the practicality of our family car, and the picturesque forest gave way to a more convenient downtown parking lot adorned with burlap-wrapped trees. Yet, amid this urban adaptation, the joy and enthusiasm endured. However, once again, the winds of change began to whisper. A decision was looming on the horizon.

"We are going to Walmart this year to pick out a lovely new artificial tree," I announced.

The reaction was definitely not what I had expected.

"What is Christmas without a real tree? Mother, what are you thinking?" Tammy and Steven demanded.

Well, Mother had done a lot of thinking. I presented my case—no more pine needles clinging to the carpet until February, no bald spots on an artificial tree, no need for watering, plus, the price of freshly cut trees was getting more expensive each year. They were not convinced. Finally, I played my ace in the hole.

I said, "Just think, each year, you will be saving a little tree's life."

That last argument proved decisive. From then on, a fake tree was the centre of activities in our home.

Our Memory Tree

Regardless of the type of tree one may have, everyone has their own ideas on how to decorate it. Some go all out with unique ornaments and baubles, others have a theme with every decoration having a shared design, while others take a more minimalist approach. The Pilon tree was different and a little more extraordinary. It had every colour and type of ornament imaginable. A gold, spray-painted macaroni tree and a beaded little man and woman made by Tammy and Steven when they were in kindergarten holds a special place on our tree, even to this day. We call it *the memory tree* as, throughout the years, ornaments made by our kids and now our grandkids are proudly displayed.

As a young wife and mother, I really enjoyed this decorating task, and I was very precise with where I would place the ornaments. I wasn't exactly anal about this job, but the tree did look quite nice when I was finished.

When the grandkids were around the ages of six or seven, they took over this job. The first Saturday in December was their time to help Grandpa decorate the tree. Chuck would string the lights throughout the boughs, place the star on top, and then the kids would attack this task with that marvellous excitement children exhibit during this time of year. In the early years, the bottom of the tree was totally loaded as far as their little hands could reach with strings of pearls, balls, icicles, candy canes, plus anything that glittered. I did not touch, change, nor add anything to their creation. As the children grew, the ornaments crept a little higher up until finally, taller kids resulted in a totally decorated tree from top to bottom. Every year, my heart would burst with joy as I watched them magically transform our tree into a piece of art, displaying all the memories of Christmases past. Life was good. Christmas was fun. And then the unexpected happened: Covid arrived.

In the blink of an eye, the world flipped upside down and everything changed. With restrictions preventing us from going anywhere or hosting visitors, the prospect of Christmas appeared rather bleak for many, ourselves included. I decided I would not decorate for the holidays, plus there would be no tree. Why bother? I told Steven of this decision.

"Mom, you have lost the Christmas spirit," he said in an accusing tone of voice.

I gave him a long thoughtful stare before I replied, "If you want spirit, in my next life, I will come back as a Christmas tree. Just think about it—the life of a Christmas tree. You only work three weeks of the year, and the fatter you get, the more attractive you look. When people walk into the room, you are instantly noticed. By just standing in a corner, you light up everyone's life. All the presents are at your feet. Did you choose them, pay for them, or wrap them? I think not, yet you get all the glory. You overhear comments such as, 'What a gorgeous tree,' and 'look at all those marvellous presents.' What's more, if you get tired and droopy, they give you a drink!"

Steven just shook his head. Once again, finding me a *home* was quickly moving up on his priority list.

But I did compromise. To prove to Steven and Tammy that I wasn't a Grinch, I decorated our seven-foot yucca plant. By placing all our memory paraphernalia on this new substitute, the special meaning of this tradition still prevailed. It looked quite festive. Furthermore, I didn't have to assemble it, nor put it back in storage. It has now become our new designated Christmas tree. An old tradition has gone, and a new tradition has been ushered in.

Winkin' On and Blinkin' Off

As I revisit past Christmases, I remember all the beautiful displays of twinkling lights on trees inside and outside of homes, in stores, and in parks. They were then, and are today, everywhere creating an enchanting, fairy-like world full of surprises and expectations. This tradition starts very early in November. Children's thrill in Christmas lights and their magic has not changed over the years. I remember taking each of our grandchildren when they were about two years of age to the mall to see the decorations. I will never forget the look on their faces as they pointed out to me each and every light they saw. I could feel their excitement. These memories are forever etched in my heart.

Because seeing the decorations and lights gave the grandkids so much pleasure, Chuck and his friend Rosaire would spend countless hours decorating our property. Lights would be put in every conceivable place possible, along with all the inflatable characters that Rosaire loved to donate. For the month of December, our place was transformed into quite a wonderland. The children loved it.

But as the grandkids got older, their fascination for our little festival of lights no longer existed. They had outgrown this type of entertainment. A decision was made. Since we had lost our captive audience, we came to the conclusion that Chuck couldn't be bothered getting the stuff out each year and I didn't have the energy to put things away after the season. So, another tradition bites the dust.

Cha-Ching: The Sound of Christmas

What would the holiday season be without the accompanying shopping adventures? My, how those experiences have evolved over the years. It's not just my attitude that has changed, but also the methods and places where I undertake this yearly tradition. I remember the sheer excitement I felt in my youth when I would spend many afternoons Christmas shopping. I had a spring in my step and a list in my hand. *Shop 'til you drop* did not apply to me then. I had energy. I had stamina. There was no dropping nor stopping me.

The arrival of the *Simpson's Wish Book* in November was akin to the Christmas trumpet sounding in our home. The sacred text of childhood dreams, the holy grail of gift-giving guidance, had arrived. Forget treasure maps; this catalogue was the real deal, capable of unveiling toys and gadgets you didn't even realize existed. Kids nationwide, including ours, would pour over this magical book for hours on end. I truly believe this catalogue was the equivalent of today's iPad.

"I *need* that and that and that," they would exclaim, pointing excitedly to at least one item per page.

"Don't you mean you *want* that," I would inquire, but this slight word distinction was lost on them.

As the holiday season drew nearer, it was time for Tammy and Steven to pare down their dream list and choose the two or three items they truly wanted. My job was to make sure these coveted items would magically appear under the tree Christmas morning—a task that sounded simple enough, and for most years, it was. However, on one particular December, simplicity was not on the agenda.

The year was 1983. Tammy and Steven's sole request to Santa was a Cabbage Patch Kid doll. This item was fast becoming the toy of the year, being advertised on children's TV programs, gracing magazine covers, appearing anywhere and everywhere kids' eyes could land. Every child wanted one. I couldn't quite grasp the attraction of this sixteen-inch doll with its plastic head, fabric body, and yarn hair, but marketing teams had surpassed themselves in promoting this latest toy craze. Each doll was unique in appearance and came with a name and a birth certificate, plus adoption papers for the recipient to fill out. For Pete's sake, the doll even bore a signature on its rear to signify its authenticity as a genuine Patch Kid.

Sensing a probable shortage of these dolls if I didn't act quickly, I began my shopping quest early in November in hopes of securing these two requested items. However, disappointment loomed large. All stores in Brampton were out of stock.

"When are you expecting your next shipment?" I asked.

"Next Saturday," was the response.

So, the following Saturday, I arrived shortly after the store opened, only to be informed once again that the popular toy was sold out. By now, desperation was starting to set in.

"When will they next arrive and where will these dolls be displayed?" I asked, pressing for every detail I could get.

I was escorted to the exact location. A large, empty table was set up, just in front of aisle four, ready to display these prized items the moment they arrived. Armed with this knowledge, I left the store with a strategy.

Two days later, I arrived half an hour before the store opened, only to see a line already forming ahead of me. Now, ordinarily, I'm a polite and considerate shopper, happy to let others go ahead of me, but not this time. No way was I going to be Mrs. Congeniality. This was war. I was determined to secure those dolls for my kids. As the doors swung open, a rush of ladies poured in, unsure which direction to head. I had the advantage. I darted past them at lightning speed and made a beeline for aisle four. There was no time to browse or select; it was a grab-and-go mission. A boy doll and a girl doll were firmly clutched in my hands. I'm not proud of my behaviour on that frenzied shopping trip, but my conduct was no worse than the other frantic women. And in the end, all the pushing and shoving was worth it. Elvis and Cecelia were greeted by two ecstatic children on Christmas morning.

Ah, the excitement, the adrenaline rush, the exhaustion, the fun of those early years.

But as time moved on, there was a shift in how I viewed holiday buying. Our kids were now adults with interests and fashions I no longer understood. Although I asked for gift suggestions, I received only vague responses from them.

"Surprise us, Mom," was their favourite answer to my repeated requests.

How helpful was that?

My enthusiasm for shopping was no longer there, but presents had to be purchased, so my attitude became: just get the job done. After finding a place to park in the back forty at the mall, I would wearily drag myself from store to store, searching for the perfect gift, only to find myself lingering at the checkout for as long as it took me to unearth the gift in the first place. The shopping experience, however, presented even more challenges. Once outside, I had no clue as to where I had parked the car. Panic immediately overtook the fatigue I had felt only minutes before. Where was that damn car? Feeling like an idiot, I briskly walked up and down the rows, frantically pushing buttons on my keys in the desperate hope that my missing vehicle would *speak* to me. This whole exhausting and stress-filled Christmas shopping ordeal was no longer fun for me; no longer my cup of tea.

"Enough is enough!" I declared, "It's high time to revolutionize this gift-buying circus!"

The solution to the ultimate gift-finding strategy was glaringly simple, practically waving at me saying, "Pick me. Pick me." I decided to take a leaf right out of Santa's playbook—after all, he had been acing the gift-giving game for centuries. If he could ask for lists, why couldn't I?

With the efficiency of Santa's elves on a tight schedule, I dispatched requests for *detailed* wish lists to all potential gift recipients—no list, no gift. Furthermore, these lists had to be very specific. Not only did I want their desires spelled out like a holiday wish come true, but I also asked for the secret map—the online store where these treasures could be found. I even suggested, "A direct link to your desired items would be oh so much appreciated."

Yes, Lynda, there is a stress-free way of gift-buying! Adaptability to change is all that is required. Armed with a glass of merlot and the power trio of wish lists, online store intel, and direct links, I have transformed into the modern-day Santa of gifting. No more chaos and no more second-guessing. I simply sit down at my computer, click away, and voilà: gifts are delivered straight to my door. The joy of gift-giving still dances through my Christmases, but, as the song goes, "I do it my way."

Gift Shopping, Man Style

Women, however, aren't the only ones who buy gifts. Men also, to some degree, participate in this activity, although, usually, there is only one person on their list: the spouse. Their wives have bought all the other gifts, including the ones for the mother-in-law.

In a way, I envy men's shopping skills. They have a whole different approach to gift buying. They don't worry about this task, nor do they plan ahead for shopping excursions, they just have a laissez-faire attitude toward the whole thing. And everything works out well for them in the end, as someone usually picks up their slack and bails them out at the last minute.

Chuck is not a shopper and never has been. For years, Tammy would do his gift buying and I did very well by her. She knew what I would like because she would ask me, plus she always came up with great ideas of her own. Chuck didn't care how much she spent as long as he didn't have to go shopping with her. Since Tammy enjoyed this Christmas activity, it was a win-win situation for all involved, especially for me. Later on, Steven took over the role of being Chuck's personal shopper for Mom.

Chuck's shopping arrangements with the kids went on for years until Covid arrived. Then, for a year or two, all personal in-store shopping was cancelled. This was seen as a blessing in disguise for Chuck. He had an excuse . . . or maybe not. Meanwhile, I was busy getting ready for Christmas by purchasing gifts online. As a steady stream of Amazon, FedEx, and UPS vehicles arrived, it slowly dawned on Chuck that maybe he better get the old girl a present. One morning, as he was flipping through the Canadian Tire flyer, Chuck asked me what I wanted for Christmas.

I was not sure where that was going, but I thought, "What the hell," and without missing a beat, I replied, "Stihl Professional BR600 Backpack Leaf Blower."

I sounded like that kid in the Christmas movie who wanted the Red Ryder air rifle. In the fall, I had borrowed my neighbour's machine to see if I could manage the weight on my back, and since I am as strong as an ox and as stubborn as a mule, two necessary qualities needed for a woman my age to carry out this task, I had handled this little puppy quite nicely, but I wasn't sure if I wanted this tool to be my Christmas gift. Not to worry. That decision was taken out of my hands.

"Phone Stewart's Equipment and see if they have one in stock," came the instructions from Chuck, "and see when we can pick it up."

Yes, the word *we* was used and most appropriately so, as *we* did pick it up.

"Merry Christmas, Lynda."

This past Christmas I devised a plan that would make Chuck's shopping for me easier. Much thought on my part was put into my wish list, which was made weeks in advance, and taped in a very prominent, can't-miss location—on the kitchen refrigerator door. I wrote this little poem to show you how well that idea worked. I call it:

Buying for the Wife

'Twas the week before Christmas, and all through the house,
Presents were wrapped, but none from the spouse.

The stockings were hung, the tree was all lit,
But nothing from Chuck, the little old sh--.

A list had been made, way in advance,
Stuck on the fridge, to see at a glance.

Tickets, events, and personal care,
All were ideas on the paper, right there.

No comment was made as the days flew by
The reason for this memo, not questioned as why.

Then out of nowhere, Chuck flops himself down.
"What do you want for Christmas? I'm going to town."

I couldn't believe, what I had just heard.
I went to the fridge but said not a word.

I pointed at the list, so clear and so bold,
"I don't want to get you those things," I was told.

"There'll be no surprise if I pick from the list."
By this time, I was clenching my fist.

The look in my eye, put wings on his feet,
"Okay," he said, "I'm off down the street."

Out the driveway he roared, in his little Ford truck.
To shop, was his purpose, this Santa Claus, Chuck.

With no list in hand, he boldly went
Returning much later, a penny not spent.

"I can't find a thing you would like," he said
While ideas from my list, swirled in my head.

"Of course," replied Chuck, "I've got a plan.
Steven, my son, is just the right man."

A call was made, and a time was set.
Arriving at the mall, two shoppers met.

"We haven't much time, so where is Mom's list?
We will look at her suggestions. Does one exist?"

"Your mother's ideas, for me, hold no appeal."
"But Dad, that is no way you should feel.

The gift is for her, and for no other.
We aren't buying for you. We're buying for Mother."

Armed with nothing but hope and a little despair,
They hustled around in the cold winter air.

From store to store, they went looking and shopping.
They were on a mission, there was no stopping.

The task was accomplished and a gift was bought,
"Lynda will like this," a pleased Chuck thought.

Arriving home, with a big grin on his face,
I knew, no matter what, I would accept it with grace.

His shopping is done, he is not empty-handed.
Chuck was relieved, I could quite understand it.

Christmas shopping is completed, with a very near miss.
But next year I'll save time and forget the damn list.

There is no denying the fact that kids bring the magic to Christmas, but women make the magic happen. But really it is the men who have the best time at Christmas. As each gift is unwrapped, and the recipient says, "Thanks Dad, Grandpa, or Chuck," he will enjoy that wonderful element of surprise as he sees, for the first time, the gift that "he" has purchased.

CHAPTER 7

THIS AGING THING

If you can't beat them at their game, reinvent the strategy.
L. Pilon

Wine, Women, and Wisdom

Amidst the wrinkles, the silver strands of hair, and the collective wisdom of countless years, we seniors have mastered the art of embracing our age with a delightful blend of humour, laughter, and a modest dash of wine. Picture this: a sunny afternoon, a charming little bistro, and a gathering of lifelong friends, including myself. This monthly luncheon ritual is a cherished tradition, eagerly anticipated by all of us. It's a meticulous affair, not just choosing the perfect venue and attire, but also orchestrating the logistics of getting there and back. Grandchildren are often our trusty chauffeurs, for some of us have parked our driving days, plus there's always a chance we'll need a designated driver by the end of this culinary escapade. Punctuality is our unspoken mantra, as no one wants to be mistakenly referred to as *the late* Lynda. The following scene depicts what transpired that afternoon.

Greetings were accompanied by hugs, and the silly question, "How are you today?" was asked.

Everyone prayed the answer would be, "I'm fine."

We were escorted to a table by a young kid who looked to be my grandson's age, but then again, at our age everyone looks young. Now, this waiter had served us before, so he was a veteran when it came to dealing with us old girls. He knew he would have his hands full, but the tip would be well worth it, plus there would be no complaints from this group, just a lot of noise. Without even asking, he immediately presented the wine list. Choices were made. The ladies on medication quickly made the decision that just this once, a glass or two of wine wouldn't hurt. Food would be ordered an hour or so later, but now was the time to drink and chat.

As the conversations and refreshments flowed, I noticed husbands were never discussed. Jokes about seniors were told, sex or lack of it was open to discussion, secrets were shared, stories of grandkids were proudly told, photos were passed around, plans for the future were exchanged, and of course, there was more laughter and more wine. The topic of our middle-aged kids came up, and I commented that they would soon be entering what is known as the sandwich years, that period between the ages of forty to fifty-nine where individuals are often put into the position of having to care for both their children and their parents simultaneously.

Many stories, both funny and sad, were shared as we looked back over the years when we were the filling in this sandwich, caught in the middle between parenting our children and parenting our parents.

"You know," I said, "there wasn't much difference between raising our kids and caring for our elderly parents."

This remark sparked a spirited conversation.

"Well," pointed out Edie, "both the young and the old have hearing issues. The seniors can't hear, and the teenagers don't listen."

"Don't forget attitude," added Susan, "Young people believe they know everything and won't be told what to do. We seniors, on the other hand, realize we don't know everything, and we simply don't care. Furthermore, we definitely won't be told what to do."

Laughter followed.

"And then there is the matter of time management," interjected Sally. "As parents, we established curfews for our kids and constantly worried when the agreed-upon time had expired without any sign of the missing child. In those days, being grounded was the punishment. Today, our kids worry when they can't reach us. They fear we *have expired*! 'I called you three times this afternoon, and you didn't answer. Where were you?' Our penalty for not keeping our kids informed of our whereabouts is the looming prospect of having to wear a medical alert device or some other type of tracking apparatus."

Heads were starting to nod in agreement. We were on a roll.

"Let's not forget about sleep patterns," Lucy countered. "Just try to get teenagers out of bed before noon on a weekend. They need their sleep. On the other hand, try to keep a senior awake past 8:00 p.m. We, too, cherish our sleep."

"Ah, don't forget memory loss," Sandra announced. "We seniors don't always remember, because we either didn't genuinely hear the conversation or, more likely, because our memory is deteriorating. Yet, when parents share information with their kids, it often goes in one ear and out the other. Why does that happen?"

"They weren't listening in the first place or deliberately didn't want to remember," was the reply.

"Drugs are an issue for both of these age groups," I said. "Remember when we worried about our kids falling into the wrong crowd, and maybe being pulled into the drug scene. Our imaginations went wild with apprehension. Where would they get the money to support this habit? Would they turn to crime? What street corner would their supplier be working on? Now, these very kids worry about our drug use."

"But if you really want to see a stash of drugs," I continued, "just peek into a senior's medicine cabinet. In most cases, these medications are government-subsidized, eliminating any need for criminal activity to afford them. Moreover, seniors don't have to stand on a street corner to meet their supplier. Their pusher, the family doctor, is only a prescription away."

There was silent agreement all around.

"Well, Mom's taxi service is still very much in demand by both kids and seniors," Sally noted with a wry smile. "While kids require transportation to hockey games and social activities, we seniors need rides to medical appointments and shopping trips."

We chuckled about the similarities between the very young and the gracefully aged, but beneath the laughter was the realization that it was only a matter of time until we would be the outside slice of bread relying on the filling to hold it together. We decided to get over these depressing thoughts. We ordered more wine.

As the wine flowed and our laughter continued, we couldn't help but reflect on the passage of time. The conversation shifted to the wisdom we had gained over the years and the advice we would offer to our children and grandchildren.

"I'd tell them to cherish every moment," said Edie, her eyes misty with nostalgia. "Life goes by so fast, and you don't realize it until you're sitting here with your friends, reminiscing about the good old days."

Susan nodded in agreement. "And I'd tell them to never stop pursuing their passions. It's never too late to acquire a new skill or pick up a hobby you love. Just look at us enjoying our luncheon and wine. We're proof that life can be fulfilling at any age."

Sally remarked, "I'd remind them to nurture their friendships. These bonds we've formed over the years are priceless. These are the friends who will be there for you when times get tough."

Lucy raised her glass, "To lifelong friendships!"

We all clicked our glasses and took a sip

Sandra leaned forward, her expression thoughtful, "I'd tell them not to sweat the small stuff. Life is too short to waste on trivial worries. Focus on what truly matters, like love, family, and happiness."

I added, "And let's not forget to appreciate the little pleasures in life. A sunny day, a good book, a glass of wine with friends—these are the things that make life beautiful."

Shirley playfully raised an eyebrow, "And, of course, always have a designated driver when you indulge in too much wine!"

Adaptation Is the Name of the Game

In the twilight of our lives, as the world around us dims, we seniors embark on an uncharted journey of adaptation. Our once-sharp senses, unwavering in their reliability, have now become fertile ground for the seeds of creativity and resourcefulness. It's a transformation born of sheer necessity. As hearing gradually retreats into the shadows, eyesight falters like a flickering candle, and memories slip through our fingers like grains of sand, we find ourselves compelled to uncover innovative pathways through the labyrinth of daily existence. I was at this crossroads, but I was up for the challenge. Ingenious solutions, or so I thought, peculiar adaptations, and an unwavering determination to embrace life's quirkiest curveballs set me in motion.

First, let me make the following profound statement: I believe I can hear better if I have my glasses on.

I know it makes no sense, but it seems to be a fact for me. After uttering this comment to my son Steven, I realized I was contributing greatly to a new exercise program he had just recently enrolled in. This particular activity improves the mobility of the neck, head, and eyes. I call it, The Eye Rolling Exercise. The only equipment required is a senior parent and one middle-aged child. This is how it works:

Senior parent: "You will never guess what I did today."
Middle-aged child: Head is slightly tilted; eyes roll to the right.
Senior parent: "And Mary said . . ."
Middle-aged child: Head is slightly tilted; eyes roll to the left.

The length of the conversation will ultimately determine the number of reps this exercise entails, but I think I'm safe in saying that my kids will have muscles on their eyeballs that will be the envy of any athlete.

This partial loss of hearing is not a new concern for us. Chuck has had hearing aids for years, but he never wears them. Once a year, he rummages through the junk drawer to locate them when the audiologist phones to schedule his annual checkup. Off he goes with aids in hand. They are definitely not in his ears. I asked him why he even bothered seeing the doctor, as he has absolutely no intention of sticking them where they were intended to go.

His answer, "I get free batteries." Honest to God he said that.

I also have a hearing issue, but it's not severe enough to warrant any further action at this time. So, Chuck and I have learned to adapt. The use of subtitles for all programs plus having the TV set at a very high volume are our somewhat successful solutions to this problem. Steven claims our TV is like a GPS. As soon as he's within a mile of our place, he is guided to our doorstep by the blaring dialogue of *Law and Order*. It works for us.

The use of a telephone, whether cell or landline, is another area where seniors have had to make adjustments to fully hear and enjoy the conversations of others. Thank God for the speaker button. I use that feature all the time.

Then just when we think we have our act together, another one of our senses, our eyesight, starts to diminish. Over the years, many of us have improved any shortcomings in this area by going through the different stages of using glasses, bifocals, reading glasses, plus other aids, and these all worked well for a very long time. Until recently, I carried a magnifying glass in my purse so I could read ingredients, directions, and the like on products while shopping. Then Tammy told me how she uses her cell phone camera to take pictures of the information she wants to read and then just zooms in for a closer look. It was a great idea, which I now use. But there will come a time when even these aids cannot do the job satisfactorily. Surgery may be the only option left. It is said that if you live long enough, you will eventually need cataract surgery. Well, I guess I have lived long enough, as I have recently had this procedure performed.

And now comes the biggie. How does the average person cope with memory loss issues? First, let me point out that there actually is a gain from this loss. Look at the amount of exercise—the steps, the stairs climbed—that would otherwise not take place if we didn't forget things.

"Why did I come into this room?"

Thump, thump, thump, back down the stairs.

"Oh yes, now I remember."

Thump, thump, thump, back up the stairs.

There must be a better reason and method for fulfilling my Fitbit's daily requirements. Maybe voicing my intentions out loud, just before moving into action, might help improve my memory.

"Lynda, you are going upstairs to get your slippers."

However, I talk to myself quite a bit as it is, and that is frowned upon by others. No sense encouraging more eye rolling.

While apps on my cell phone have helped me see and hear things better, it's the phone's camera that really wins the gold star for helping me deal with memory issues. On our recent holiday, I took many photos for a variety of different reasons.

As Steven was flipping through this massive collection, he asked, his voice tinged with curiosity and a hint of bemusement, "Mom, why do you have a picture of the front of a bus with the number 223 prominently displayed in its window?"

"Well dear, there were over twenty tour buses all looking alike at the rendezvous point for pickup and I wanted to make sure your dad and I got on the right one."

Eyes started twitching, not knowing whether to move to the right or to the left.

"Mom. Why do you have this picture of intersecting street signs?"

"Well dear, our hotel was located at that intersection, and I wanted to remember the street names in case we needed to ask for directions."

Eye movement went into full motion. I then grabbed the phone out of his hands and pointed to a picture of Chuck.

"See that picture of your dad," I said. "I took it, so I would remember which old man to take home with me."

The eyes did not move.

Sometimes we seniors just have to take a stand.

Is Mom Ready for the Home?

Do you have a bucket list? It's possible that many individuals under the age of fifty-five might not be familiar with this concept. The other day, as I sat gazing out my kitchen window, lost in thought, it hit me. Time was slipping by, and perhaps creating a bucket list for myself should be a priority. Oh sure, in the past I had jotted down tasks and goals, but they were mostly mundane to-do lists, lacking the excitement and daring adventures that a bucket list should encompass. How boring. Well, time to change that.

While I searched for a pen and paper, it occurred to me that brilliant ideas might flow more freely and easily if I had a glass of wine for a companion. So, after pouring myself a generous glass of merlot, I eagerly sat down to draft my agenda.

"What will I put on my list?" I thought, "What do I still want to accomplish in this lifetime?"

After much thought and a great deal of wine, I came to the conclusion that my bucket would not only overflow with fun events but more importantly, at least once a year, there would be an activity that wasn't appropriate for a senior my age to consider. This was the criteria. The ideas poured quickly onto the paper. I proudly showed the *Lynda List* to my kids, who immediately vetoed most of the events and ambitions I had outlined.

"Mom. A hot air balloon ride? For God's sake, you're afraid of heights."

"An African lion safari. Do you want to be eaten alive by lions or insects? Take your pick."

"Mom. Ziplining? Are you crazy?"

In their eyes, I was simply hastening my trip to *the home*, but what do kids know? I was in my seventies, so it was definitely high time that I started checking off a few items.

Now, women my age were raised during a modest time when only the daring wore a bikini, so it was quite bold for me to even consider this venture: getting a bikini wax. I must confess I have never owned a bikini, nor do I have any intentions of making this purchase in the near future, but what the hell, it was time to cut loose. Live a little, face new challenges. I had been a client at Amanda's Spa for many years, so I had complete confidence in her ability to provide this service.

Upon entering her establishment, I immediately sensed a wave of tranquility washing over me. The subtle, gentle lighting, the soft background music, and the assurance of complete privacy had the power to soothe even the most hesitant of souls. Clad in nothing more than a G-string, I took my place on the waxing table, a testament to the boldness of my resolve. As Amanda mixed the wax for this undertaking, I detected a slight, mischievous grin on her face.

"Lynda," she asked, "May I discuss your waxing experience

with my students in my class next week?"

Permission was naively granted. I felt relaxed. Ignorance, they say, is bliss, and I embraced it wholeheartedly. I stared at the ceiling as Amanda applied the very warm wax using a popsicle stick. I will never quite look at a popsicle the same way again. She then fanned the area, so the wax would harden.

"I will only do a small area at a time," she said. "That way it won't hurt."

The wax hardened. She RIPPED off the wax. Now imagine a fat frog with his eyes bulging out because someone had stepped on his back. You have just pictured me.

After I climbed back down from the ceiling, I realized there were still a few more areas to go, plus there was the other side to this story. But I was prepared now. With eyes squeezed shut, I was as rigid as a board. The job was finally completed.

"Now," said Amanda, "Heat will open up the pores and irritation may occur, so for the next twenty-four hours, don't do anything that will cause heat or friction, like wearing tight undergarments, exercising, or sex." (Honest to God, she said this.)

What sacrifices one has to make. But the experience was worth it. Been there, done that, don't ever want to do it again.

Leaving Amanda's Spa, a rush of exhilaration surged through me. I had dared to take a leap, embracing an experience my children would never anticipate nor approve of. I realized there are moments when veering from our children's counsel becomes not only enticing but essential. Maybe ziplining, going on a wildlife safari, or perhaps a serene balloon ride was in my future? The choices remained tantalizingly uncertain, but one thing was sure: my appetite for adventure had been whetted, and I was ready for the next adrenaline-charged challenge.

Footnote: I couldn't wait to tell Tammy and Steven that maybe now I should buy a bikini, since my body was prepared for this occasion. I didn't know that they could shudder that violently.

Saving One's Sole

In the turmoil of recent years, seniors like us found ourselves in uncharted territory. We weren't just wrestling with the trials of aging; we were also thrust into a whirlwind of technological advancements, all thanks to the pandemic. While some of these changes left us bewildered, one thing was for certain: our new reality demanded adaptation. For some, this transformation was a struggle, while others embraced it with ease, and then there was Chuck, a man of untold talents, who had a unique, quirky way of evolving into this new way of life.

In the blink of an eye, our tried-and-true methods of shopping, banking, communicating, and learning became relics of the past. Cheque books gathered dust, and cash was met with skepticism. Credit and debit cards became the currency of everyday life, even for the simplest of purchases like a cup of coffee. Online banking was hailed as a marvel, and e-transfers were the lifelines for sending money. Zoom meetings and webinars took centre stage, rendering the need for arduous journeys to see guest speakers obsolete. Heck, you didn't even need to change out of your pyjamas. Just grab a cup of coffee, settle into your living room, power up your computer, and presto! You had the best seat in the house for that virtual lecture. I must admit, this new way of learning had its charm.

During the Covid era, I wholeheartedly embraced online

shopping. The allure of curbside pickups or doorstep deliveries was undeniable. No more tiresome queues, no crowded stores, and no more trying to recall where you'd parked your car. It was almost perfect. Yet, there was one item in my view, which couldn't be bought online: footwear. Shoes demanded a personal test for fit and comfort before any commitment could be made. However, like most women, I had a closet full of shoes, so I didn't fret too much about not being able to buy a new pair immediately. It seemed Chuck wasn't concerned about acquiring new shoes, either.

One day, he made a peculiar request. "Where is the Gorilla Super Glue?" he inquired.

Now, I have learned not to question these odd requests in case he might give me an answer. In one hand, he cradled a pitiful, dilapidated shoe, its toe and sole gaping miles apart, and in the other hand he held a C-clamp. I thought, at the time, perhaps the kindest thing to do would be to just throw the shoe away and put it out of its misery, but I kept this opinion to myself. I watched in disbelief as he meticulously glued the sole of this poor, worn-out boot and then attached the C-clamp tightly to its toe, resulting in a tight embrace between it and the sole. However, Chuck's mission was far from over.

"I need the stapler. Where is it?" was his next question.

Without uttering a word, I handed him the requested tool. The Velcro fabric was expertly stapled back onto the adjustable strap.

"Good as new," he proclaimed, with an unmistakable note of satisfaction in his voice.

When in-store shopping restrictions were eventually lifted, we made a trip to the store in search of a new pair of shoes. However, did Chuck part with the old pair? Goodness, no! Those old shoes, worn and torn, remained in our possession on the off chance that the new ones might hurt his feet.

And so, as I reflect on this rollercoaster ride of adapting to the digital age amidst the chaos of recent years, Chuck's remarkable shoe-saving skills serve as a fitting symbol of our resilience. While we navigated the uncharted waters of online banking, virtual lectures, and curbside pickups, his determination to mend his beloved shoes reminded me that sometimes, the old ways can still hold value in our ever-evolving world.

Undercover Shopping

I can't genuinely tease Chuck about his lack of interest in shopping, as I too despise this activity, particularly when it extends into the realm of clothing. The pandemic, with its stringent regulations, which practically mandated a lack of dressing up or going out, had unwittingly provided me with the perfect excuse for wearing old, comfortable attire. However, as the world regained momentum during the recovery phase, and rules and restrictions were gradually eased, I came to a stark realization: I could no longer put off this looming task. My wardrobe practically cried out out for a transformation, imploring me to get something new and fitted, no more baggy pants and t-shirts.

However, my hesitation wasn't solely born out of procrastination; it was rooted in the frustrating reality that nothing ever seemed to fit or flatter my figure. Stylish clothes appeared to be designed exclusively for tall, slim women. My five-foot frame, adorned with bumps and lumps in all the wrong places, presented its own set of challenges. It was high time that I embarked on a quest to discover what would look good on my apple-shaped figure so that it looked less like . . . well, an apple.

My research led me to an intriguing solution: proper undergarments. Allegedly, these mystical pieces of clothing could work miracles, instantly shedding ten pounds, banishing muffin tops and love handles, delivering impeccable tummy control and boob support, transforming you into a vision of confidence and beauty in mere seconds, and God knows what else. Well, I'm not gullible, but I was desperate, so I thought it wouldn't hurt to check this crazy theory out.

First on my agenda was a bra-fitting session. Apparently, if *the girls* hang down to your belly button, clothes will have a hard time tucking in at the waist. This session was quite the experience and thank goodness the salesclerk was female. I had no idea I was wearing the wrong size for all these years. Once everything was properly in place, we proceeded to the domain of midsection management.

Muffin tops, I was informed, were not the ideal companions for jeans. Solutions to this problem ranged from compression garments and shapewear, to bodysuits and Spanx—different names, but all trying to achieve the same purpose: to create the illusion of a slimmer silhouette. The thought crossed my mind that perhaps it was the intense workout you did while wiggling in and out of these damn contraptions that might bring about a slimmer you. The elastic in these things would put a loaded slingshot to shame. I could not believe this high-waisted, mid-thigh piece of equipment came with step-by-step instructions on how to get into your knickers. It sounded almost obscene. And God help you if you need to go to the bathroom while wearing this restrictive outfit.

Finally, my mission was accomplished. I was now outfitted with expensive undercover items no one would see. Furthermore, my budget definitely needed to be reworked. I was tired, worn out, and fed up with the whole shopping ordeal.

Back home, I once again tried on my purchases, and as I looked in the mirror I thought, "Oh for Pete's sake Lynda, go put some clothes on."

As I peeled off this new, confining, costly lingerie and slipped back into my old comfy pants and sweater, I couldn't help but chuckle at the absurdity of my undercover shopping adventure. Sometimes the pursuit of style and the quest for the perfect fit can be quite a challenging journey. And then it hit me. Good Lord. Unless I had aspirations of posing for Playboy in my seductive undies, or baring *all*, wishing to join a nudist camp, more shopping on my part was imperative.

I was teetering on the brink of panic. I needed stylish clothes people would actually see me wearing. How was I going to accomplish this task? And then I remembered a suggestion I had stumbled upon during my research: the idea of having a personal shopper by my side. This concept intrigued me. While store clerks could offer assistance, their motivations often leaned toward sales, leaving a gap in understanding my lifestyle and unique fashion needs. Could I trust them to provide honest feedback on an outfit's suitability, or were their compliments merely a sales tactic? And the all-too-familiar frustration of their sudden disappearance when needed most lingered in my mind.

So, I thought, "Who could be my trusted shopping companion?"

I envisioned someone with a keen sense of fashion, a passion for selecting fabulous clothing, and the ability to deliver honest assessments with a touch of diplomacy. I craved feedback that didn't bluntly declare, "Lynda, you look awful in that outfit," but instead offered a kinder, gentler, "That style just doesn't do you justice."

I needed someone with a fresh perspective, perhaps someone outside my age bracket, to breathe new life into my wardrobe. Enter the perfect candidate who effortlessly met all my criteria: my friend, Leanne.

My sole directive to her was concise: "I want clothing that doesn't make me look like a little old lady."

Fortunately, this posed no challenge for Leanne, who was in her element. She was organized and ready for the challenge, having decided prior to our shopping day which boutiques met my needs.

Through Leanne's urging, I tried on outfits I would never have given a second look at if I'd been on my own. The off the shoulder top looked good on this old girl, and that pair of elegant evening slacks created a slimming effect that did wonders for me.

"Lynda, you have great-looking legs. Show them off," she suggested. (God bless her.)

A pair of dressy shorts was added to the mix.

Laden with boxes and bags, and accompanied by a profound sense of accomplishment, our shopping excursion ended. That day I learned two things. Firstly, there are many great alternative methods one can use to tackle often-dreaded chores, and secondly, don't abandon the routines that have worked for you in the past.

"Now, Leanne," I said, "we have one more task to do. Let's relax with a glass of wine."

If All Else Fails, Just Wave

In the midst of my mature years, I've come to appreciate the art of forgiveness, especially when it comes to forgiving oneself. This revelation struck me like a bolt of insight while strolling through the bustling mall the other day.

As I passed a group of young mothers, I overheard one exclaim, "I could have died of embarrassment!"

A knowing grin crept across my face, and I couldn't help but think, "Young lady, you have no idea how many *deaths* of embarrassment lie ahead in your journey through life."

Embarrassing moments—we've all danced with them at some point in our lives. They are the cringe-inducing, soul-flushing episodes that make our cheeks flush and our hearts race. But as time passes, something magical happens. Those mortifying instances transform from scarring memories into humorous anecdotes, shared and cherished with friends and strangers alike. I have had my share of embarrassing escapades, from the days of feeling utterly stupid, to feeling a little silly, to embracing the notion that sometimes, the best response to life's absurdity is a hearty laugh, not just at the world, but at oneself. These self-inflicted blunders, and the profound wisdom they unfailingly yield, become the threads expertly woven into the intricate fabric of one's existence.

The Feeling Stupid Years

It was the 1960s, the hazy days of my youth, when mini-skirts were in and cigarettes were still a fashion statement. Chuck and I were on our way to a wedding in Sudbury when I realized my cigarette supply was at a dangerously low level. Unfamiliar with the area, Chuck stopped at the first place we came to. As I entered the establishment, I found myself in a seedy bar that felt like a page out of a gritty novel. And there I was, all dressed up, looking very much a young lady, wading into this den of characters, who probably had either just gotten off the night shift at the mines or didn't work at all, slouched on their bar stools, drinking beer. The minute I walked in, the room came alive with wolf whistles and naughty comments that sent my cheeks into a fiery blush. I just wanted to grab my cigarettes and make a swift exit.

In the late sixties, cigarettes in many establishments, especially bars and restaurants, were dispensed from machines just like candy bars. I immediately made a beeline towards the machine and hastily put my coins in. I hit a button and the music blared. To my horror, I realized I had unwittingly triggered the jukebox. Forget about the cigarettes. I turned and fled. I had made those patrons' day. Not only did I give them a hearty laugh about what I had done, but I also left them with a song to listen to. I felt totally stupid and humiliated. But then I realized that I would never see them again and maybe, just maybe, they were too intoxicated to remember the incident. Those thoughts made me feel a *little* better. Today, I would have handled the situation very differently, but back then, I was a young, naïve farm girl from another world.

The Feeling Silly Years

Fast forward to the 1970s, when the weekly visit to the hairdresser was a ritual for every woman in town. Now, if you slept just right and used enough hairspray, you could maybe make it to your next appointment with every hair still in place. However, on the off chance your hair became a mess, say on day five, you had that situation covered. Wigs would tie you over for those extra two days. These hair contraptions were hot and ill-fitting, but at the time, they were the best available and everyone owned one, including me. If you had a bad hair day, you simply stuck on the wig. I was teaching school during this era, and I usually needed a wig day twenty-four hours before my next hair appointment. I remember this particular day so well.

My class of eight-year-olds was lining up to go back into the school after recess. Pushing and shoving like all kids do, they more or less made their way into line in an acceptable manner, except for one child: Brent. This kid was big for his age, was the one who misbehaved in class, and I loved him dearly. He had spirit. Brent wanted to be first in line, so at breakneck speed, he arrived like a baseball player sliding into home plate. As he came to a screeching halt, he accidentally bumped me, making me lose my balance. Although I didn't fall, the jolt did something very comical; at least that is how the kids saw it. Off flew my wig, landing at my feet. There was dead silence from this boisterous group. The kids thought I had been scalped. I bent down, picked it up, and plunked it back down on my head.

Trying to ease their shock and surprise, I made the comment. "Brent has finally made me blow my top." Tension eased and laughter followed, including mine.

For the rest of the day, I had a very happy class. Smiles and giggles could be periodically heard throughout the room.

It appears this incident would become legendary; a tale recounted at dinner tables across the town. Word travelled fast, and soon, even acquaintances in the grocery store were greeting me with the comment, "I hear your wig fell off at school."

The power of a good laugh, even at oneself, knows no bounds.

The What the Hell Years

Moving from a crowded, busy city to a rural property had a beautiful, calming feeling my body and soul craved. Nature had so much to offer, and there was nothing behind our house but farmland and trees as far as the eye could see. Blinds and curtains were not installed on these windows because I wanted nothing to block this tranquil scene. Let the sun pour in and nature unfold. Well, this philosophy worked for a while, but then one morning I learned an important lesson. As I looked out my bathroom window to admire the beauty of the back fields, I realized you should not do this when you are stark naked, especially when you have given permission to cross country skiers to use those fields. Well, what else could I do? I waved.

So, I say to those young mothers I encountered at the mall, "Life is a series of embarrassing moments, but as you journey through it, these moments will transform into cherished memories filled with laughter and fondness. You will not just survive; you will thrive and revel in the comedy of it all."

The Aging Test

As I navigate the winding road of my senior years, I often find myself caught between the youthful spirit in my heart and the unmistakable signs that time is marching on. Like most seniors, I don't consider myself old. In our minds, we're still in our forties, planning adventures and chasing dreams. Our bodies may whisper the passage of time, our faces may be etched in wrinkles, but our hearts remain young and defiant. We refuse to be defined by a number, and we certainly don't behave like we're inching closer to our supposed expiry dates. And when it comes to keeping our families guessing, well, let's just say that I've made it an art form.

As I reflect on the routines and habits that have quietly crept into my life, it becomes evident that I may be further along the timeline than I'd like to admit. Take, for instance, the fact I now read the daily obituaries, a habit most seniors share. While younger generations are busy checking their Facebook pages for updates on their friends, we seniors check the *Passed-book* (obits) to see the status of ours. So, really, it's not so different, is it? The other day, as I perused these, I came across someone who had passed away at the age of seventy-eight.

I caught myself thinking, "Well, he lived a good, long life."

Suddenly, it hit me like a ton of bricks: "Holy hell, he was only a year older than me. The guy died young!"

You see, as a teenager, everyone seemed ancient. When I approached thirty, those over fifty were considered elderly. But as I crossed the threshold of sixty-five, a reverse way of thinking began to take hold. Suddenly, those older than me seemed remarkably youthful. Eighty became the new prime, eighty-five was seen as 'a little older,' and perhaps, just perhaps, that ninety-year-old was truly 'old.'

I enjoyed my fifties; the kids were through university, and any extra money was ours to spend on ourselves. Turning sixty-five meant I no longer had to ponder the qualifying age for senior discounts. Was it fifty-five, sixty, or sixty-five? It didn't matter, I qualified for them all.

It is rather interesting to note that once you hit your seventies, your children become concerned that 'Mom is starting to *lose it*.' For example, if you forget something, it's attributed to aging or even the dreaded spectre of dementia. But when they forget things, which happens more often than not, it's simply because they're 'busy, busy, busy' with a lot on their minds. During these years, your kids may feel the need to look out for you, a gesture that can be both endearing and, at times, downright annoying as hell.

An example of this concern for my well-being happens when my family comes over for dinner. The first thing my kids do is stick their heads into the fridge to see if any items there have gone past their due dates. They have even passed this duty of food inspector on to their kids. When staying with me for holidays, the grandkids will often say, "Grandma. Is this still good to eat?"

And I simply reply, "If it isn't growing a coat of fur, it should be fine."

Because they love to devour food and Grandma hasn't poisoned them yet, they accept that answer.

I have thought a lot about this *aging thing*. Was I closer to my mythical age of forty, the age I feel in my heart, or was I, in fact, my biological age? To find out, I decided to make a checklist of all the things I've started doing or observing lately regarding my behaviour. The results were eye-opening. My age meter was definitely heading upward.

Here is my list:

You might be old if . . .

- your cardiologist looks younger than your grandson.
- the first thing you do each morning when the newspaper arrives is read the obits.
- you and your friends discuss which funeral home serves the best egg salad sandwiches.
- you find a Kleenex tucked up inside the sleeve of your sweater.
- someone calls you "Ma'am." (I hate this)
- the hairs have left your eyebrows and have migrated down to your chin.
- you start a conversation with the words, "Now, stop me if I've told you this before."
- your grandkids don't believe a word you say about your childhood.
- you use your good china dishes instead of paper plates at special family gatherings.
- you can't remember the name of the person you were introduced to just a minute ago.
- you not only know and recognize all actors over the age of seventy, but you also can name all the movies they starred in.
- you are the only one in your family who has a landline.
- you see expensive antiques and you realize they were in your childhood home.

- you have to check your cell phone to see which day it is.
- dinner is served at 5:00 p.m. sharp and not a minute later.
- your entire social calendar consists of medical appointments.
- you can laugh at and identify with all the old senior jokes.
- you catch yourself doing things or saying things which remind you of your father.
- Facebook has an object where you have to guess its name and use, and you realize you have one in your cupboard.
- your body has more new parts than old, used ones.
- you have to decide whether it is worth the effort to bend down to pick up an object, or to just leave it and trip over it later.
- you ask your young grandchild to help download a new app on your iPad.
- people are wearing clothing that was stylish in your youth, and now they are calling it retro.
- you send letters using snail mail.
- your communication skills are out of whack. Grandkids can't read cursive writing, and you don't understand their shorthand texts – LOL, TGIF, LMAO, etc.
- you get distracted while in the middle of a sentence, and you can't remember what you were talking about. Even more embarrassing is the fact the person you were talking to can't remember what you were saying either.

- you put something in a safe place, and later you can't remember where that was.
- you start taking pictures on your phone to remember where you parked the car.
- you turn down an invitation to a party because it doesn't start until 9:00 p.m.
- you spend half your day looking for things.
- you need an afternoon nap so you can go out that night and play cards with friends.
- the most common topics discussed with your friends are operations and medications.
- you have an entire kitchen cupboard holding nothing but prescription drugs and medical supplies.
- you realize there is so much you don't know, but at this stage in the game, you really don't care
- your mind and body are not on the same page. Mind says, "You can do it." Body says, "No, you can't."
- you wonder what idiot is phoning you at 9:00 p.m. Don't they know you are in bed for the night?
- you have the TV at its highest volume level, plus the subtitles are being displayed.
- your back goes out more than you do.
- your kids start to parent you.

It doesn't really matter how one scores on this little exercise, because in the grand scheme of life, our aging process weaves a narrative that's unique to each of us. It's true; you might be old if you recognize the quirks and nuances that come with the passage of time. If your cardiologist looks younger than your grandson, if you cherish the daily ritual of scanning the obituaries, or if conversations with friends turn to the best egg salad sandwiches at funeral homes, you're on a journey filled with tales of a life well-lived.

There's wisdom in finding a Kleenex tucked up your sweater's sleeve, and resilience in facing a world that sometimes addresses you as "Ma'am," though you may loathe it. The migration of eyebrow hairs to your chin is a badge of honour, as is the wisdom that prompts you to say, "Now, stop me if I've told you this before."

And what about those grandkids who question your childhood stories? They are the testament to the ever-evolving world, where your experiences stand as bridges across generations. As you choose the cherished china over paper plates and explore the realms of forgotten memories, you remain the keeper of time's secrets.

Yes, you might be old if you need your cell phone to remember the day, if dinner is served at 5:00 sharp, or if your social calendar is filled with medical appointments. The laughter shared over old senior jokes is a symphony of shared experiences, and as you catch yourself echoing your father's words, it's a reminder that the past is not forgotten.

The world may marvel at retro fashion, while you treasure letters sent through snail mail and decipher the shorthand of younger generations. Lost sentences and hidden objects are but small detours in a life filled with cherished moments and discoveries.

And in the twilight years, you'll find joy in taking afternoon naps to prepare for nights of card games with friends. The cupboard may hold prescription drugs and medical supplies, but it's also a repository of resilience and adaptability.

For in the end, what defines your age is not the list of quirks and changes, but the spirit that keeps you ticking; the fire that refuses to burn out. So, let's discard the notion of an expiry date, for life is meant to be embraced, cherished, and celebrated. In the face of time's steady march, you remain the captain of your journey, steering towards new horizons, and there's no age limit to living life to the fullest.

ABOUT THE AUTHOR

Lynda Pilon, a proud wife, mother, and grandmother, resides in Southern Ontario with Chuck, her husband of fifty-six years, and a small troop of endearing cats. After a mere seven decades of gathering life experience (and cat hair), Lynda authored her first book. This is her second literary adventure, both published in her late seventies—proof that it's never too late to unleash your inner author or start a new chapter in life!

Manufactured by Amazon.ca
Bolton, ON